European Competition Policy

Keeping the Playing-Field Level

European Competition Policy: Keeping the Playing-Field Level

Published by Brassey's for Centre for European Policy Studies,
33 rue Ducale, B - 1000 Brussels (Director: Peter Ludlow)

Also available from Brassey's

The Annual Review of European Community Affairs 1990, edited by Peter Ludlow

The Annual Review of European Community Affairs 1991, edited by Peter Ludlow, Jørgen Mortensen and Jacques Pelkmans

German Unification in European Perspective, Wolfgang Heisenberg

Setting European Community Priorities 1991-92, edited by Peter Ludlow

The Future of Pensions in the European Community, edited by Jørgen Mortensen

CEPS Papers

50 *North-South in the EMS: Convergence and Divergence in Inflation and Real Exchange Rates*, by CEPS Economic Policy Group

51 *From Centrally-Planned to Market Economies: Issues for the Transition in Central Europe and the Soviet Union*, by Daniel Gros and Alfred Steinherr

Forthcoming titles in 1992

The Annual Review of European Community Affairs 1992, edited by Peter Ludlow, Jørgen Mortensen and Jacques Pelkmans

Setting European Community Priorities 1992-93, edited by Peter Ludlow

The Treaty of Maastricht, by Peter Ludlow

Forthcoming CEPS Papers

Europe and North America in the 1990's – Peter Ludlow

The European Union after Maastricht: Rhetoric and Reality – Peter Ludlow

European Community Trade Policy after 1993: The Case of Textiles and Clothing – Jacques Pelkmans

CEPS publications are available on subscription and in single copies. The annual subscription includes 6 CEPS Papers, the *Annual Review of EC Affairs* and *Setting EC Priorities*.

Subscription orders: Turpin Distribution Services,
                            The Distribution Centre, Blackhorse Road,
                            Letchworth, GB - Herts SG6 1HN

                            Telephone   (0462) 672555
                            Telefax   (0462) 480947

European Competition Policy
Keeping the Playing-Field Level

Sir Leon Brittan

Published by Brassey's for CEPS

BRASSEY'S (UK)

First English edition 1992

UK editorial offices: Brassey's, 165 Great Dover Street, London SE1 4YA
orders: Marston Book Services, PO Box 87, Oxford OX2 0DT

USA orders: Macmillan Publishing Company, Front and Brown Streets, Riverside, NJ 08075

Distributed in North America to booksellers and wholesalers
by the Macmillan Publishing Company, NY 10022

Library of Congress Cataloging in Publication Data
available

British Library Cataloguing in Publication Data
A catalogue record for this book is available from the British Library

ISBN 1-85753-077-2

Printed in Great Britain by The Bath Press, Avon

Contents

Preface

This book is based on a set of lectures delivered at CEPS between July 1991 and July 1992. Sir Leon has added another (chapter 12), delivered to the London Common Law and Commercial Bar Association.

The idea of this lecture series came from Sir Leon himself, and I must admit that when he first proposed it, both my senior colleagues and I were sceptical about the feasibility or appeal of twelve "official" statements of policy over such a short period. Our doubts were, however entirely misplaced. The series was a major success, both in terms of attendance and, as readers of this book will be able to testify, in terms of contents.

At a time when the Community system is under criticism for being less than transparent, it is a particular pleasure to publish a book that gives such an elegant example of explanation and persuasion. I hope that in the early part of 1993, when the responsibilities of the new Commissioners have been drawn up, I can persuade one of Sir Leon's colleagues to perform a similar task with regard to another area of EC policy.

Peter W. Ludlow
Director, CEPS

Brussels, October 1992

1. Introduction

Competition Policy is a somewhat slippery concept whose scope is the subject of considerable debate. As a general matter, however, I view competition policy as encompassing more than the various anti-trust rules contained in the EEC Treaty and elsewhere. To confine it to that narrow a spectrum would be to remove almost entirely the element of "policy", in the sense of the systematic pursuit of particular objectives. On the other hand, competition policy is not so wide as to sweep in any measure or goal which relates to or affects the free operation of market mechanisms. Such a broad notion runs the considerable risk of confusing a host of interrelated, but separate, policies and would make it impossible to follow any coherent aims. I prefer to view competition policy as embracing the objectives and means which are set and used within the Community for the purpose of allowing firms to vie with each other for customers in an integrated market, and which protect the competitive process from the imposition of public or private restraints.

As the Commissioner responsible for Community competition policy, I have often been cast in the role of the "big bad wolf" standing in the way of private transactions and practices, as well as saying no to a variety of market intervention measures adopted by Member States, most notably state subsidies. What I shall try to do here is to explain the nature of EC competition policy, to comment on its applications and scope and, hopefully, to make clear why I take the positions I do.

Foundations and guiding principles

I am ever conscious that I have inherited responsibility for a system with an impressive constitutional pedigree. The founding fathers showed considerable foresight in grounding the Community competition scheme in Treaty rules. Not only have these rules, as part of the Community's highest law, been accepted by twelve Member States with widely varying traditions, but the rule of law has been reinforced by the existence of a firm set of principles which can only be altered by means of an amendment to the Treaty itself. Neither I, nor any of the competition Commissioners before me, write competition policy on a clean slate. Rather, we come to a structure whose broad contours have been in place for some time and whose architecture we must respect.

The Treaty defines competition policy in terms of both objectives and means. As for objectives, Article 2 of the Treaty sets forth an ambitious set of goals which revolve around the concept of a common, integrated market designed to promote the development of economic activity and to increase living standards. The existence of a system of "undistorted competition" as a prerequisite for the achievement of such a market is confirmed in Article 3. The means for creating this competitive environment are set out in detail in Articles 85-94, provisions whose role I will consider in a moment. The basis of these articles is the protection of a system of competition which encourages efficient production, technical progress and fairness toward the consumer.

Thus it is that the Treaty lays out firm objectives and consistent policies. Individual company practices and agreements, as well as state schemes and grants of financial assistance, must be assessed in the light of these rules.

The central goals of market integration and the promotion of vigorous competition have consistently been stressed by the Commission. Over a number of years, in its annual reports on competition policy to the European Parliament, the Commission has fleshed out the terse Treaty provisions in order to provide as much guidance as possible to individuals, companies and Member States. So it was that the first Report declared that "the Community's policy must, in the first place, prevent governmental restrictions and barriers which have been abolished from being replaced by similar measures of a private nature". This idea has been re-emphasised in Reports in intervening years. Most recently, the 20th Report remarked: "Member States must not be allowed to replace forms of protectionism abolished in the market-integration process by state aid or exclusive rights accorded to monopolies. Companies must not be allowed to thwart integration [either]".[1]

The goal of a single market has been given new momentum in the context of 1992. It is now widely accepted that the benefits expected to flow from an internal market presuppose the existence of a system of healthy competition, where firms are free to vie with each other for customers by offering the highest quality product at the best price. It should not be assumed, however, that the goal of 1992 has somehow changed the nature of competition policy. It has not. Rather, it has served to give new impetus to our implementation of policy and to educate both industry and governments on the crucial role of competition in Europe.

It is clear, therefore, that one of the principal aims of competition policy is that of altering the structure of the markets within which competition takes place. This approach is one which results in important differences between EC competition law and the law of other jurisdictions. The Community puts particular emphasis on the elimination of vertical restraints and territorial restrictions which tend to divide up markets. There is a strict policing of intellectual property licences and, in order to prevent the isolation or elimination of small or regional firms, the Commission "welcomes co-operation between small and medium-sized enterprises where such co-operation enables them to work more efficiently and increase their productivity and competitiveness [in] a larger market."[2]

---

1. Commission of the European Communities, *XXth Report on Competition Policy* (Brussels/Luxembourg, 1991), p.11.

2. Commission Notice concerning agreements, decisions and concerted practices in the field of co-operation between enterprises, *OJ* 75/3, 29 June 1968).

However, it would be wrong to think of EC competition policy merely as an instrument designed to bring about structural change. Rather, the promotion of "competition" as a process and an economic system is inextricably intertwined with the goal of market integration. This concept is evident from the Treaty itself and is again explained in greater detail in the Commission's Competition Reports. As stated in the 1989 Report: "An effective competition policy means that firms will have constantly to maintain a high level of efficiency and competitiveness, and can no longer rest on their laurels." Such efficiency will lead to better products, better service and greater innovation. The promotion of competition compels firms to offer the lowest prices to customers and this helps to raise standards of living. It is no accident that the wealthiest and most productive nations on earth are those whose markets are based on free competition.

Thus, competition policy makes a contribution to the Community far beyond the elimination of trade barriers. It is the champion of the consumer. Cartels to raise prices are rooted out and struck down. Companies are not allowed to divide up markets and consumers are free to buy goods and services throughout the Community. In recent times, the Commission has intervened to break up "horizontal" agreements between a manufacturer and the distributors of its products (e.g. Toshiba) which distorted price competition and separated markets within the EC.

The combined goals of achieving an internal market and promoting competition create a form of competition law which does not fit in neatly with any particular school of economic analysis used in other jurisdictions. For example, the "Chicago School" approach currently in favour in the USA is not directly relevant to EC competition policy. Chicago does not need to worry about creating a single market. Rather, it presupposes the existence of an integrated market.

This is certainly not to say that EC competition policy rejects an economic approach. Far from it. The Commission and the Court of Justice consider that the application of a strictly economic approach is perfectly compatible with the Treaty goals. Economic analysis is indeed essential in any competition-policy consideration. Markets must be carefully and correctly defined, costs must be identified and calculated (e.g. for predatory pricing) and the impact of a given transaction on competitive relationships and market structure must be assessed. Moreover, I have consistently emphasised that the application of the Merger Regulation[3] will be designed to prevent the growth or creation of firms which might abuse market power by raising prices. The economic underpinning of this analysis is clear.

It may be true that, over the years, as the goal of market integration is achieved, the role of economic analysis will take on an even greater degree of importance in the formulation and implementation of specific policy. This is an idea which I shall develop in a later chapter.

---

3. Council Regulation (EEC) No. 4064/89 of 21 December 1989 on the control of concentrations between undertakings, *OJ L* 395, 30 December 1989.

In sum, then, the principal components of competition policy are clear. They are laid down in the Treaty and have, as we will see, been expanded on by the Community institutions. Moreover, the stable foundations of the policy have helped us to avoid the politicisation of decisions and the comings and goings of intellectual fashion in anti-trust analysis.

The application of competition policy

As mentioned earlier, along with general principles the Treaty sets forth, in Articles 85-94, a more concrete expression of the Community's competition policy. These provisions provide the instruments whereby any private agreement, unilateral action or state subsidy which might interfere with a system of "undistorted competition" can be prohibited or notified.

Thus, saying no is a fundamental part of administering competition policy. The best way of arresting the undesirable effects of an anti-competitive practice is not to issue warnings or to request that guidelines be followed. Rather, the practice should be stopped so that the interests of the consumer and of the "system" of competition are protected. Indeed, I would be acting in derogation of my duty if I were to permit any arrangement to proceed which would retard progress to the Single Market, erect private trade barriers, enable a firm to abuse its dominant position to the detriment of the consumer or permit a Member State to provide unjustified subsidies to firms.

Complaints that Brussels is too interventionist, or is impeding the ability of firms to compete on the international scene, almost invariably come from the companies who are not permitted to act as they wish or from Member States who are told they cannot give the subsidies they had planned. These complaints highlight the fact that they have been told "No". But it should never be forgotten that, in the application of competition policy, saying no to one party necessarily implies saying yes to someone else. The merger that is prevented saves a competitor from extinction. The cartel that is exposed ensures a level playing-field for other firms. The state aid that is prohibited ensures fairness for those who would not receive such money or help.

Moreover, the Commission will only outlaw those parts of an agreement which contravene Treaty provisions. It may well be possible to allow a merger or practice to proceed which should otherwise be prohibited, provided it is accompanied by other measures leading to a net increase in competition. For example, the recent acquisition by KLM of 80% of the shares of the Dutch airline Transavia was allowed to proceed only on the basis of a commitment by the national authorities that the combined airline would be open to effective competition, clearly defined by reference to the routes it would fly. A similar result was reached in the Air France case in 1991. A number of mergers which have been reviewed under the provisions of the new Merger Regulation have been cleared subject to certain provisions which will ensure the existence of competition with the new firm. The question is one of achieving the right balance.

While the Commission has a wide range of instruments at its disposal, in their application can be discerned the essential principles of competition policy mentioned earlier. The policy is evident in the following areas:

a) *Merger enforcement.* Recognising that a company which is allowed to achieve a dominant position can then act in an anti-competitive manner and divide up markets, the Commission is able to prevent the achievement or strengthening of such a position of dominance. Indeed, the preamble to the Merger Regulation makes clear the policy goals which are to underline its application. For example, the goal of creating a single market is thrown into clear relief by the market-definition issues presented in each case. I will discuss this in greater depth in a later chapter.

b) *Article 85.* When companies collude and agree to apply restrictions which interfere with the free operation of the market, it is often to the detriment of the consumer and can run counter to the notion of a single market. Article 85 is the expression of Community policy that such agreements should only be permitted where there are direct benefits for the consumer. Otherwise, such agreements are void. Most recently, the Commission imposed a fine on Toshiba for its practice of prohibiting exports of its photocopiers between Member States. I shall discuss the procedural aspects of Articles 85 and 86 in the next chapter.

c) *Article 86.* Again, in the light of the goals of competition policy, the contours of Article 86 are readily understood. The potentially-detrimental effects of abuses of the competitive process are highlighted by the recent court judgment upholding the Commission's Decision that the chemical company AKZO had acted improperly when it moved to eliminate a competitor by pricing a particular chemical below cost. The unfairness of this tactic is apparent and competition policy was able to ensure that the existing market balance was not unlawfully disrupted.

d) *Article 90.* This is proving to be a useful instrument for the introduction and expansion of competition on an industry- or sector-wide basis. For example, in the telecommunications sector the Commission has sought to put the "products" in question on a more competitive footing, in that key national monopolies have been removed. The aim is to open up the market, promote efficiency and ensure that consumers receive better service and lower prices.

e) *State-aid policy.* The goal of protecting competition also demands that the Commission prohibit subsidies which would provide a firm with unfair advantages. In general, companies in the EC's internal market should compete fairly with each other, not with each other's taxpayers! Beggar-my-neighbour subsidies undermine competition, the internal market and the Community's regional and cohesion policies. On the other hand, aid which enhances competitive performance (such as research and development aid) may well be compatible with competition policy. Also, the market-integration goal militates in favour of regional aid when it clearly promotes cohesion in the Community, by helping disadvantaged areas catch up.

Thus, the common threads of policy can be seen running through actual decisions of the Commission and the Court.

Although competition policy is based on firmly-established principles, it is not static in the sense that a particular practice or subsidy, if it has once been considered compatible or incompatible with Community goals, will necessarily be considered so in the future. Rather, the application of the policy takes account of changing circumstances and technologies. For instance, in its moves to liberalise the telecommunications sector, the Commission has not dismantled national monopolies in the area of voice telephony. This is to ensure that this vital service is provided to consumers on a continuous basis. However, if technology were to develop to a degree where a universal network could be assured without national monopolies, or if it was determined that the existence of such monopolies significantly retarded competition in other important areas (such as electronics), the Commission would have to rethink the current position. Thus, the application of the relevant articles of the Treaty is far more like applying the provisions of a constitution than, say, construing a revenue statute.

Flexibility is also evident in the structure of Article 85 itself, which permits the giving of exemptions limited to a period of time. The process whereby such exemptions are renewed allows the Commission to look again at the competitive structure of the market to which the exemption applies. Also, while the Merger Regulation does not permit the Commission to put a time limit on its approval of a concentration, it would always be open to the Commission to use Article 86 to challenge the practices of a company which had become dominant since the merger creating it was approved. Thus, just as markets are subject to change, competition policy is sufficiently flexible to take account of such changes.

There is of course ample room for debate about specific elements of competition law and policy. I realise that such topics as co-operative and concentrative joint ventures, market definition and state-aid policy are subjects for lively and sincere debate. I might consequently be persuaded to change a particular rule or policy, but what I attempt to do in administering the competition portfolio is to apply clear and coherent rules to cases before me, to announce guidelines where appropriate and in this way to enhance the application of the rule of law. If there is to be change in some particular area, because we feel that such an alteration would better serve our overall objectives, then the change will be made in as clear and as reasoned a manner as possible.

The scope of competition policy

While the importance of competition policy for the success of the Community is firmly established, it is not the only means identified in the Treaty for the achievement of a common market. It is also vital that the Community should have coherent agricultural, regional, and transport policies, and so forth.

Indeed, the competition rules themselves acknowledge that factors other than "pure" competition can sometimes be of overriding importance. For example, Article 85(3) provides that, even if an agreement between firms distorts competition "within the common market", it may nonetheless escape the automatic prohibition of Article 85(2) if it promotes "technical and economic progress" and allows consumers a fair share of the benefits which the agreement brings. Also, Article 90(2) acknowledges that certain companies, which have been entrusted by a Member State with the operation of a service of general economic interest, may fall outside the rules on competition if the application of such rules would obstruct the company in the performance of the tasks assigned to it. Finally, Article 92 acknowledges that certain forms of state aid are not incompatible with the common market, although they must by definition distort competition.

The common feature of these exceptions is that they are part of the overall structure of competition policy. They are contained in the chapter concerning "Rules on Competition" and they represent relatively limited derogations from the principle that the consumer and the Community are best served when public and private restraints are eliminated from the market-place.

It is also clear to me that competition policy cannot ignore the other policies which are essential to the Community. For example, the Commission recently approved funding arrangements for Britain's Channel 4 television which will provide a financial safety-net guaranteeing the channel a certain level of advertising revenue. The intention is to avoid the danger that direct competition for advertising with ITV might dilute the quality of Channel 4's broadcasts. The Commission considered that this approach was compatible with the Community's broadcasting *and* competition policies.

This form of recognition of other policies is wholly proper and appropriate. What competition policy cannot be asked to do, however, is to become an instrument of another Community policy which is regarded as having greater priority. For example, there are those who might argue that we should use competition policy as a means of building up strong "national" or "European" industrial champions, or that the rules on the grant of state subsides should be relaxed so as to permit the protection of "strategic" or failing industries. Such courses of action cannot be permitted. It would not represent an "adaptation" of policy; it would be an abandonment of policy altogether. Moreover, such a course of action would ignore the significant evidence that healthy domestic competition is one of the main factors in producing healthy international competitors.

Competition policy cannot be forced into a role for which it is not suited and which would ultimately retard the progress toward a Single Market and put consumers at risk of being dominated by lethargic companies. That is the antithesis of what the Treaty requires of me.

The effective application of competition policy is also limited by the scarcity of resources at our disposal. There are only so many cartels we can investigate, so many decisions under Article 85 we can adopt each year and so many state-aid schemes we can review. I would not want to give the impression that anyone is being allowed to get away with anything, but it is a simple fact that we cannot do everything as quickly as we would like.

Nonetheless, we make every effort to make the law and policy clear. It is to be hoped that this clarity will enable national courts and private litigants to take the initiative in applying Community law themselves. Strong national enforcement would be a welcome ally in the implementation of Community policy.

Conclusion

The continuing integration of the Community, and the ever-present need to protect the consumer against competitive abuses, ensures that competition policy will always play a vital role in Europe. The policy will continue to encompass prohibitions on conduct, as well as positive measures. We must resist the temptation to warp competition policy for the sake of imagined gains on other fronts. It is abundantly clear that the scheme laid down in the Treaty, a scheme which has stood the test of time and changing circumstances, serves to benefit us all.

2. Procedures

An effective competition policy is vital for the successful implementation of the single market programme, but policy cannot be made in a vacuum. The principles of EEC competition law are not self-executing. Without active and effective procedures for enforcement, competition policy itself would be no more than the expression of pious aspirations.

From the very beginning, the enforcement of the competition rules has been one of the most important instruments available to the Community for promoting economic integration. The attraction of this system of competition law lies, I think, in its simplicity. Article 85 contains a clear prohibition of agreements and concerted practices which restrict competition on the Community level, subject to exemption in certain specified circumstances. Similarly Article 86 is very clear in its absolute prohibition of abuses of dominant position. In both cases, the general prohibition is backed up by powerful sanctions and effective powers of investigation.

The primary responsibility for enforcing those rules was put squarely on the Commission. Regulation No. 17, passed thirty years ago, established the Commission as the guardian of the principles of free competition enshrined in the Treaty and gave it the means to enforce those principles.[1] Besides the largely administrative task of clearing notified agreements, the Commission was given active powers to investigate suspected infringements of competition rules and to impose fines and cease-and-desist orders.

In the intervening years Regulation No. 17 has been criticised on occasion, but it has stood the test of time. I would like to pay tribute not only to the foresight of the Community's founders for setting up a system which has worked so well over the years, but also to the ingenuity and inventiveness of those in the Commission who have built on our existing powers and adapted them to suit changing needs.

As we accelerate towards the goal of a single market, our vigilance in enforcing competition law has also increased. By making effective use of our existing enforcement powers and by building upon them, we have been able to ensure that the full benefits of the internal market are not frustrated. First, we have continued to direct our efforts against "classic" infringements of Articles 85 and 86, namely market-sharing and price-fixing cartels and serious abuse of monopoly power in major industrial sectors. We have also successfully implemented the new Merger Regulation, which establishes the Commission as the authority empowered to regulate mergers with a Community dimension. We have strengthened our procedures against illicit state subsidies and we have

---

1. EEC Council: Regulation No. 17: First Regulation implementing Articles 85 and 86 of the Treaty, *OJ* 013, 21 February 1962.

begun to introduce competition into regulated industries, an area from which up to now it has been largely absent.

Articles 85 and 86

The acquisition of our new responsibilities, particularly the immense challenge of implementing the Merger Regulation, has not meant that the Commission's activities in other spheres of competition enforcement are in any way diminished. As recent fines show, the Commission is still very much in the business of investigating and imposing sanctions on anti-competitive agreements and practices. The Tetrapak case is the latest in a whole series of decisions in which it has taken firm action against companies which flout the competition rules in important industrial sectors. Cartels have been discovered, and heavily fined, in the soda ash and polypropylene sectors and regarding a number of other important chemical products.

I am particularly pleased that the long saga of the AKZO case came to an end in July 1991, with the Court of Justice substantially upholding the Commission's decision under Article 86 to fine the Dutch multinational for unfairly trying to force a small but inconvenient competitor out of business. The internal market is for everyone, big or small.

What is absolutely clear is that without the vigorous use by the Commission of its investigative powers, conferred by Articles 11 and 14 of Regulation No. 17, few of these cartels and monopoly abuses would ever have come to light. In several recent cases the "smoking gun" evidence was found during unannounced investigations ordered by decision and carried out simultaneously across the Community. It would certainly never have been produced on a voluntary basis by any of those involved in the clandestine activities. The power to make surprise investigations has always been there in Regulation No. 17 but for many years went largely unused. Most inspections were made by prior notice and we handled few hard-core cartel cases. During the last ten years, however, the Commission has increasingly had to use such measures in investigating major cases. The press has dubbed these investigations "dawn raids" - something of a misnomer because they always take place during normal business hours. The rather dramatic impression given of a sudden swoop by Commission agents also tends to obscure the fact that it is only by painstaking thoroughness and professionalism on the part of the officials carrying out the investigations that the incriminating evidence is discovered amongst masses of company documentation and records.

Given the Commission's record of success in investigating cartels, it was no surprise to us that some very determined challenges to its powers have been made, both inside and outside the Court. I am glad to say that they have proved unsuccessful. In the National Panasonic case in 1980, the European Court of Justice upheld our power to order and carry out investigations without warning the companies beforehand. The firm involved had advanced the curious proposition that a surprise investigation was such an intrusion into its commercial privacy that notice should be given in advance. Since that time, it has generally been recognised in legal and industrial circles that this power is a necessary one. Even so, recently our investigative powers under both Article 11 and Article 14 have again been challenged in the Court. These procedural appeals were made in the plastics cases which ultimately resulted in heavy fines being imposed under Article 85.

In the Hoechst case, the firm refused to submit to the investigation: it argued that our investigation under Article 14 amounted to an illegal "search" because it had not been authorised by judicial warrant. Of course we have never claimed the power for Commission officials to enter a firm's premises by force or against its consent. Such direct steps could only be taken under the enforcement measures which each Member State is obliged to adopt under Article 14 (6) of the Regulation and which are designed to ensure that our investigators can get in. Without such measures the Commission itself can only apply indirect persuasion - fines and periodic penalty payments. The right we did claim - and one which the Court upheld - was the right, once a firm submitted, to carry out an active examination of its files and records, to look for the evidence ourselves and not be confined to one room.

At the same time as Hoechst, the Court was called upon to decide in two cases whether there was a "right to silence" entitling suspect firms to refuse to provide information requested under Article 11. Had such a right been allowed, it would have made Article 11 a dead letter. Again the Court largely upheld our powers. It recognised that the whole point of Article 11 is to enable the Commission to obtain information on suspected infringements, and the firms suspected of being involved in a violation are probably best placed to provide useful information about it.

It is perhaps ironic that some of the opposition to the Commission's investigative powers has come from legal and business groups in my own country. No one can deny that in the United Kingdom the powers of the authorities to investigate cartels are limited. They do an excellent job with what they have. For years, however, the Director-General of Fair Trading and others have been pressing for the same investigative powers as the Commission. It is unfortunate that the Government has not been able to find parliamentary time for the necessary legislation. But there has been remarkably little disagreement that it is much needed.

So far I have talked about the powers of the Commission at the investigative stage. The Commission, however, does not only investigate infringements of competition rules: under the scheme of Regulation No. 17, it is called upon to decide the case itself. This combination of functions has also attracted a critical reaction: it is claimed that the Commission is policeman, prosecutor, judge and jury all rolled into one. Of course it might have been conceivable, when the Treaties were being drafted, to provide for the Commission to prosecute cartel violators before some neutral judicial body. As a barrister, I would have felt very confident of obtaining a "conviction" in a competition court on the basis of the evidence which we have found in our investigations. That option was not, however, taken up and our procedure became an administrative one. Recognising that it was through decisions in concrete cases that competition policy would best be developed, the founding fathers of the Community entrusted the Commission with the function of deciding - as well as investigating - cases of suspected infringement. There is of course nothing unusual or unfair in administrative law in conferring original jurisdiction on a competition-enforcement agency. The Federal Trade Commission in the United States is just one example. What is important is that before taking its decision, the authority should give the parties affected a fair chance to be heard. Our procedures fully incorporate the *audi alteram partem* principle as it is familiar to common lawyers. Indeed, in many respects our procedures go beyond the requirements of English and American law in ensuring the fairness of the decision-making process. Once it has been decided there is sufficient evidence to start the case, a very detailed Statement of Objections is sent to the firms. All the documentary evidence on which the accusation is based is disclosed to them. They have the opportunity to reply in writing to the case against them and also to present their defence and call witnesses in an Oral Hearing. The legal and factual issues are canvassed exhaustively before any final decision is taken by the Commission, we consult the Advisory Committee from the Member States, and of course the decision itself has to be very comprehensively reasoned.

Despite these built-in guarantees, firms appealing to the Court against our decisions frequently allege a whole string of examples of the Commission's alleged unfairness. Often the Court rejects these complaints: they usually turn out to be no more than a procedural quibble, although I fully understand and respect companies which choose extensive grounds of appeal. Insisting on the "administrative" nature of the procedure, the Court will only overturn a decision if the alleged irregularity has involved some real prejudice to the applicant. Critics of our procedure have seized upon this "administrative" label to claim that the Court is thereby giving its seal of approval to some second-class standard of justice. They demand that our procedures be made more "judicial". I am afraid that those who advocate such reform have been beguiled by the terminology. As the Court has stressed, "administrative" and "judicial" are not mutually-exclusive concepts. The fact that an authority is an administrative body does not free it of the duty to act fairly. In deciding what this duty of fairness requires, one has of course to take account of the way the procedure works. You cannot just take the complex procedural rules appropriate to a criminal trial in a court of law and graft them unchanged on to an administrative body like the Commission applying economic law. Of course, we already have a code of procedure for our cases in Regulation No. 17 and other legislation. To those who say that the Commission should be subject to a more detailed and rigid set of procedural rules, I would reply that what matters is the *substance* of administrative justice. The Commission's procedures in investigating and taking action against serious violations of competition law have certainly proved effective: but they are also very fair.

I would like to say a word on the subject of fines. Under Regulation No. 17, infringing firms can be fined up to 10% of their previous year's turnover. I regret to say that some firms seem to regard our fines as just another overhead. We are still uncovering large cartels in major industries and in some cases the same firms have been involved on several occasions. The impact of the fines obviously has yet to work its way through to the boardroom and the Annual General Meeting. A fine of 10 million ECU seems large in absolute terms but it may represent a tiny fraction of a firm's total turnover. The latter figure may well give a better indication of the firm's commercial power and its ability to pay. In the summer of 1991 the Commission imposed a fine of 75 million ECU on a single-product company. Multi-product industrial combines cannot safely think that they will continue to be treated more leniently if they engage in hard-core cartel activities. Whether a company manufactures one product or a hundred, the message is the same: serious violations of Community competition law will be punished by high fines.

Merger policy and procedures

As we approached the deadline for the completion of the 1992 programme it was widely agreed that a single market needed a single merger policy. The practical problem we faced in the late 1980's was that the application to mergers of the existing provisions on competition was unclear. The Treaty of Rome - unlike the Coal and Steel Treaty - was entirely silent on the whole question of mergers. Over the years, however, we had been able to use the existing provisions - Articles 85 and 86 - to deal with some forms of concentration which presented a threat to competition - another example of the adaptability of our rules. In the Continental Can case, the Court of Justice upheld our use of Article 86 to prohibit a merger which enhanced a pre-existing dominant position. More recently the Philip Morris case pointed the way to the application of Article 85 to some forms of concentration. That case involved one company acquiring an influential shareholding in a competitor.

But at best the existing rules were limited and technically inadequate for a proper merger control policy. It was not clear even after the Philip Morris case how far Article 85 could be applied to full takeovers. In any case, in a hostile bid the necessary element of agreement would seem to be lacking. In such a case we might have been able to apply Article 86, but only if the takeover resulted in the abuse of a dominant position. There were also problems of potential conflicts of jurisdiction, and the absence of any obligation to notify could have pre-empted any efforts on our part to intervene at the right stage.

I must say that my predecessor, Peter Sutherland, performed sterling work in extending the frontiers of the existing framework and intervening to good effect in a number of mergers which presented a threat to competition. But it became increasingly clear that, however well we were able to build on our existing procedures, we needed a single, clear instrument for merger control on the Community level. The draft Merger Regulation had remained blocked in the Council for sixteen years, and unanimity always seemed beyond our grasp. It was thus particularly satisfying when we were able to secure agreement for the

1989 Merger Regulation. I believe that one of the factors which finally spurred the Member States into agreeing to giving us the power to control large-scale mergers was the reputation we had built up in other fields as a responsible and effective enforcer of competition policy.

The Regulation itself is firmly based on competition principles. There had been a tendency in some quarters to view merger control as an instrument for governmental intervention in industrial and social policy, empowering the authorities to determine the size and location of industry and to build up European champions to take on United States and Japanese competition. I am glad to say it was finally recognised by all that *dirigisme* of this type was outmoded and counter-productive.

It should be stressed that our policy objective was never to discourage the merger process as such: many mergers are neutral or even enhance competition. The policy embodied in the Regulation was to meet the need of industry for rapid decisions on the basis of clear-cut rules and procedures, while at the same time protecting European citizens and consumers from concentrations which imperilled competition.

Given the complexity of the issues involved, I think the Regulation has established machinery which is swift, clear and, above all, effective. In the first place the Commission is established as the authority with exclusive jurisdiction for controlling mergers with a Community dimension. It was clearly essential to establish the single regulatory-control principle in European merger policy. Companies intending to merge had to know whether to apply to the national authorities or to the Commission for clearance. This object was achieved by defining clear turnover thresholds to draw a line between Community and national jurisdiction. Putting it broadly, the Commission has exclusive jurisdiction in concentrations involving firms with an aggregate worldwide turnover of 5bn ECU, and an EEC turnover of 250m ECU each, unless two-thirds of the EC turnover of each undertaking is in one and the same Member State. The turnover figures in these thresholds will, I hope, be reduced in due course to 2bn and 100m ECU respectively. The single regulatory-control principle has resolved one of the most vexing problems in controlling proposed mergers, namely double jeopardy and the risk of a conflict between different jurisdictions. The exceptions to the principle have so far not been successfully invoked.

We have also clearly defined the operations which fall within the Merger Regulation. This was essential because we provided for a system of compulsory notification backed up by substantial fines. Once a concentration falls within the criteria it has to be notified to the Commission for vetting. I should point out that there is a very useful provision for confidential discussions prior to any formal notification: this informal pre-notification procedure has proved invaluable both in assisting parties to decide whether they have to notify and in directing our attention to the principal competition issues.

Our procedure is very swift. Strict deadlines have been laid down. Within just one month we have to decide whether or not a validly-notified concentration raises serious doubts as to its compatibility with the common market. The regulation lists the facts which the Commission must take into account when making this analysis. If we have no serious doubts, a positive decision follows. As we predicted, this has proved to be the case with the majority of proposed mergers. The enormous advantage to industry of a rapid examination by a single authority based on competition criteria alone cannot be underestimated.

If there are serious doubts, a further analysis becomes necessary. Formal proceedings have to be opened and must be completed within four months. Once again, subject to limited exceptions I have referred to, the Commission's decision is final throughout the Community, although of course like all Commission decisions it is subject to judicial review.

Our merger procedure has also proved extremely effective. So far we have received 48 notifications and have cleared 41 of them within one month. Five cases have moved on to the second phase of investigation. The two exceptional cases above the thresholds, where the competition authorities of the Member States might have jurisdiction, have given rise to no conflict. The basic principle of the Regulation, that no Member State should claw back cases which we had already decided, and which presented no special grounds for local consideration, has been respected.

We have thus set up a simple, clear and workable procedure for Community merger control, with the Commission responsible for cases above the thresholds and the Member States for those below. The fact that the Member States were willing to confer this vital jurisdiction upon the Commission sends a clear message to the world: the Community is committed to a strong and independent system of merger control.

Procedures in regulated industries and cases of state aid

I now turn to two fields in which the Commission has fashioned the instruments to deal with competition problems despite the fact that we had no detailed procedural regulation laying down our powers.

Regulated industries
In the past few years we have succeeded, by our policy of vigorous enforcement, in breaking down many of the barriers to intra-Community trade created by companies themselves. Many industrial sectors which had slumbered in the mistaken belief that they were free from the rigours of competition enforcement have received an abrupt awakening. But it is in those markets subject to state regulation that effective competition has been most noticeable by its absence.

Article 90(3) is the provision which enables the Commission to ensure the respect of Article 90 by addressing decisions and directives to Member States, and the European Court of Justice has upheld the Commission's prerogatives in this regard. Article 90 provides for the full application of the Treaty rules, including those on competition and the free movement of goods and services, to companies owned by or in a special relationship with Member States, except where the application of such rules would prevent them from carrying out their public-service obligations.

The upholding of the Directive on telecommunications terminal equipment has pointed the way to opening up the market in many other regulated sectors where competition has hitherto been lacking. We are going to adopt a very active policy of implementing the various Treaty rules. Each sector will be studied on its merits but our activity in this important area will be increasing in the near future. In particular we will be pursuing in a variety of ways our campaign to complete the internal market in energy. As a mark of our seriousness in this regard, only recently we prohibited an agreement between Dutch electricity companies which inhibited electricity imports. We have also taken action to challenge import and export monopolies for electricity and gas in several Member States.

State aid

So far I have dealt with our anti-trust procedures in relation to the activities of companies and regulated industries. But there is another area where it was essential for us to develop appropriate procedures to maintain a competitive environment. Many of the benefits which flow from effective application of the competition rules and the creation of the single market would be significantly undermined if Member States were free to support companies by providing unjustified state subsidies. This artificial form of funding could significantly distort competition in the common market and place the non-recipients of aid at a distinct disadvantage. It also creates a dependency culture which is the antithesis of a healthy competitive climate. For this reason the Treaty provided, in Articles 92-94, for the control of state aid. Member States are normally required to notify such aid to the Commission, which has then to decide whether the grant in question is compatible with the common market. Where it is found incompatible, the Member State may be required to cease all such aid, and the Commission may require it to be repaid.

It soon became apparent that a strict control of state aid was vital for the success of the 1992 programme. As the various obstacles to internal trade are dismantled, such as differences in standards and discriminatory public procurement rules, subsidies are one of the last means available to governments to shelter local industries from competition from elsewhere in the Community.

Soon after I took up my duties in Brussels, I set in train a comprehensive review of our policy in the state-aid sector. The three main directions in which we concentrated our efforts were: achieving transparency about the real levels of aid being granted; taking strong action against the most anti-competitive and wasteful subsidies; and rolling back the general level of aid.

During our review we discovered that the levels of aid being granted to manufacturing industries were disturbingly high, and were often being given to producers located in the most favoured and prosperous areas of the Community. Such unjustified measures completely undermined our policy of helping peripheral regions through the Structural Funds. I was therefore determined that as 1992 approached we would use our full enforcement powers under the Treaty to ensure a level playing-field, not only against newly-notified aid, but also to schemes of continuing subsidies approved many years ago and which had grown out of control.

In contrast with the cartel and merger fields, there is no implementing regulation in the state-aid sector. This has not, however, given rise to uncertainty as to the necessary procedure or the criteria on which the Commission decides. The basic principles are set out in Articles 92 and 93, and the Court of Justice has, in a series of judgments, clarified a large number of outstanding questions, both procedural and substantive. The Commission has also issued decisions and policy frameworks setting out both substantive and procedural rules.

One serious problem which we did face was the failure of some Member States to notify the Commission of subsidies, in clear breach of their obligations under Article 93. In other cases Member States have been reluctant, even when pressed, to provide the information necessary for a proper examination by the Commission. Even if we did ultimately obtain the details of such unlawful aid, the time at which we could usefully intervene might be long past and the damage irreparable. On a number of occasions we made known our concern regarding these cases. The recent judgment of the Court in the Boussac case has gone a long way towards providing the Commission with an effective means of policing illicit subsidies.

In cases where aid is granted in infringement of the obligation of prior notification, we will apply the following procedure. We will first require the Member State to supply full details of the aid in question within 30 days, or even less in urgent cases. If the Member State fails to reply, or provides an unsatisfactory reply, we will adopt a provisional decision requiring it to suspend the application of the aid within 15 days, and initiate the procedure under Article 93(2) to make it provide all the data necessary for us to assess the compatibility of the aid with the common market. If the Member State still fails to comply, we may adopt a final decision of incompatibility on the basis of the information in our possession and require repayment of the amounts unlawfully paid. Should the Member State fail to comply with the interim or final decisions, we can refer the matter directly to the Court of Justice. I hope and expect that as a result of these new procedures, and the steps we have taken to inform the Member States of our policy and procedures, there will be a greater awareness on their part of their obligations under Articles 92 and 93.

Finally, I must mention the Commission's most recent procedural decision on state aid, which is of considerable economic and industrial importance. In July 1991 the Commission decided to introduce annual monitoring of the financial flows between public authorities and publicly-owned companies. From now on, Member States will be required to submit each year a financial statement for all public companies with a turnover of more than 250m ECU in the manufacturing sector. The information received will allow the Commission to decide whether aid is involved in that financial relationship - for example, if there is no, or an inadequate, return on capital. This procedural device will enable the Commission, for the first time in a systematic way, to ensure that public and private companies are placed on an equal footing and that there is no distortion of competition arising from their capital structure.

As Commissioner responsible for Competition Policy, I fully support recent proposals to amend the EC Treaties so as to permit the imposition of appropriate fines on Member States which flout their obligations under the Treaty rules. Such a sanction would be of particular usefulness to secure compliance in the two related fields of state aid and regulated industries. I doubt whether it would be in the scheme of the Treaties to provide for the Commission itself to impose the fine, but I would have no objection to our bringing a case before the Court of Justice and recommending an appropriate fine.

Conclusion

In recent years the Commission has established for itself a reputation as one of the world's leading anti-trust enforcement agencies. Our armoury of rules and procedures for dealing with restraints on competition has now been complemented by the new powers to control mergers. In the context of the process of the integration of the Community, the Commission will continue to use all the legal and procedural instruments at its disposal to ensure that the rules and principles of competition are respected. Competition will be maintained and safeguarded in those areas where it already exists. In particular, we will continue to prosecute hard-core cartel activity and blatant cases of monopoly abuse. It may be that we will have to redouble our efforts in this area of competition enforcement.

In other sectors where competition is less than vigorous because of state intervention, we will ensure that firms do not forever remain sheltered from the invigorating breeze of competition. Innovatory measures will be employed where appropriate to achieve this purpose. My officials in Directorate-General IV are vigilant defenders and enforcers of competition and they do not lack ingenuity. They are also keenly aware that the realisation of the single market depends to a large extent on a healthy and effective policy of enforcement.

3. Merger control

The Council adopted the Merger Regulation with the conviction that it was imperative that the control of certain concentrations be carried out at the Community level. I believe the Commission's initial experience shows that this conviction was well-founded.

There are two aspects to this. I shall examine why our experience has shown that merger control at the Community level is necessary, and also why the Regulation itself constitutes a valid instrument to undertake this task.

The vast majority of the 54 concentrations notified to date[1] have concerned cross-border deals. This shows that the Council's choice was valid on substantive grounds. Of the 51 decisions, only 7 concerned mergers of companies from the same Member State. Concentrations with Community-wide effects require a market analysis of similar scope. The focus of merger control at national level will inevitably be limited to the effects of the operation in the territory of the country in question. A concentration should only be prohibited on competition grounds if it results in the merging firms having an unacceptable degree of market power on the relevant geographical and product markets. Those markets must be defined according to economic, not political criteria. To look at the effects of a concentration in a single Member State when its effects and true economic context are Community-wide must lead to incorrect and unreliable decisions.

Furthermore, the importance of fact-finding at the Community level in such cases should not be underestimated. The basis of any analysis of the effects of a merger on competition rests on a determination of the existence of substitutes for the products of the merging firms. A regulatory authority must identify the actual and potential competitors of the merging firms to determine the extent of their market power post-concentration. Such an analysis rests on a number of structural factors and on market research. It is of crucial importance to take into account the views of those directly affected by the concentration. In order to correctly delineate markets and assess market power, considerable fact-finding is therefore necessary. Potential substitute suppliers for goods of the merging firms often lie outside a single Member State, as do potential customers. The need for a regulatory body with the mandate and tools - in particular linguistic - to undertake the necessary research is clear.

The Tetra Pak/Alfa-Laval case is a good example of this. Tetra Pak was dominant in the market for aseptic liquid-packaging machines. It was acquiring Alfa-Laval, a major producer of milk- and juice-processing machines. The Commission had to decide whether the ability to offer both packaging and processing machines under a single aegis would strengthen or create a dominant

---

1. September 1992.

19

position on either of these two markets. Most of the structural factors indicated that such a dominant position would indeed be created or reinforced. However, the Commission undertook a very detailed inquiry, consulting over 60 companies in all 12 Member States. This showed that in reality the packaging and processing markets were rather distinct, and that no creation or strengthening of a dominant position would result from the proposed takeover.

The trend for concentrations to have economic consequences wider than a single country is not limited to the Community. Some have effects worldwide. There is a real need to liaise with other regulatory authorities in relation to such operations if there is a risk of conflict. This is better undertaken centrally by the Commission than individually by a number of Member States, as was shown during the first year of the Merger Regulation's operation. The Commission maintained close contact with the Swedish authorities in the Tetra Pak/Alfa-Laval case, and with the Canadian authorities in the Aérospatiale-Alenia/De Havilland case.

The recent EC-US agreement[2] is a significant advance in this respect. It provides an effective mechanism for avoiding, whenever possible, conflicting decisions. It contains a notification procedure, provisions for the exchange of information, and a procedure for discussing cases of mutual interest. A major new development is the inclusion in the agreement of both positive and negative comity provisions. Both authorities take fully into account the interests of the other party in their decision-making, according to a defined procedure and a specified set of relevant considerations. This relates not only to situations where one authority would wish another to refrain from acting, but also when it would wish the other to take enforcement action. The agreement should be welcomed not simply for these conflict-avoidance provisions, but also because it establishes a forum for discussion of the wider issues of merger policy. These discussions will no doubt assist the continuing moves towards convergence of merger policies worldwide.

With respect to convergence, Europe itself is making important and rapid progress. The recent EEA Agreement[3] will bring merger control onto a common footing between the Community and the EFTA countries. The Europe Agreements with Czechoslovakia, Hungary and Poland envisage the adoption in these countries, over time, of competition rules based on those of the Community. A trading block of more than twenty countries with common anti-trust rules is thus within sight in Europe.

Prior to the entry into force of the Regulation, anxieties were widely expressed that its complex procedures and tight deadlines would make it a cumbersome and inappropriate instrument. It is generally recognised that this has not been the case.

The single regulatory-control principle, another important reason for the Council's decision to institute merger control at the Community level, has worked well. The Commission alone has vetted all concentrations with a

---

2. 23 September 1991.

3. 22 October 1991.

Community dimension since September 1990. Concerns that the principle would be defeated by national-authority "meddling" have proved wholly unfounded. Most of the twelve Member States now have merger-control provisions, and some concentrations not having a Community dimension have required participants to notify or inform all of these authorities. The reduction in expense and lost management time resulting from a single filing at Community level is popular with businesses. The Council's belief that merger control at a Community level was necessary for this reason has also been vindicated.

The substantive implementation of the Regulation recognises that the economic system of the EC is based on the principle of the free play of the open-market mechanism as the best way to determine resource allocation. It is not bureaucrats, but entrepreneurs making production and marketing decisions in reaction to millions of consumer purchasing decisions, who decide how to use available resources. The constant striving for profit maximisation leads to innovation and ever-increasing efficiency. The maintenance of effective competition ensures that the benefits of such innovation and efficiency are passed on to consumers.

As a rule markets are dynamic and self-correcting. Even a firm with a large market share will often be forced to remain innovatory and efficient to retain that position. The Commission will be concerned when a proposed concentration is likely to make it impossible to preserve the discipline that effective competition imposes on firms. The formulation of a merger-control policy based on this principle does not lead to a conflict between European Community industrial and competition policies. Both of these policies are based on the principle that markets work. Consumers and companies are best served by competitive pressure leading to innovation and efficiency, not by dominance. One might be able to point out certain short-term benefits to companies that acquire market power. Experience, however, has shown that these benefits are transitory, as well as expensive for the consumer. For European companies to prosper and grow, the discipline of a competitive Community market is indispensable.

The Commission's interpretation of the merger-control regulation, and in particular the concept of dominance as it relates to single-firm market power, reflects these basic principles. Dominance is "the ability to act to an appreciable extent independently of competitors, customers, and ultimately of consumers". This definition was first established by the European Court in 1978, and is as valid today as it was then. However, the first year's experience has shown that whether merging firms will in fact have the ability to act independently can be difficult to determine.

The Commission approaches the problem as a two-part analysis. Firstly, it defines the markets in which the companies compete, and then it assesses their power in those markets. The determination of the geographical reference market presents the Commission with a number of difficulties that are particularly relevant in the European Community.

The continual integration and interpenetration of national markets means that Community markets are in a state of flux, moving gradually from being national to Community-wide in scope. Defining geographical reference markets in these circumstances is particularly difficult. The Commission approaches this problem from a pragmatic standpoint, examining whether the conditions of competition between different geographical areas are homogeneous. It may ask the question whether, as a matter of fact, imports or exports *would* flow between countries in response to increased demand. This is an entirely different question from whether they *could* do so, and reflects a determination on the Commission's part to approach merger-control analysis from an economic, as opposed to a political perspective.

The CEAC/Magneti-Marelli case provides a good example of this problem. No legislation exists preventing the import and sale of batteries into France. Thus, one might expect the geographical reference market in this case to be wider than a single Member State. However, when the Commission examined the problem, it discovered that, due to consumer brand-loyalty and the lack of a cross-border distribution and marketing infrastructure, imports would not be likely to enter France in response to an increase in demand. More likely, the price would increase. The market was thus considered national. Many Community markets have developed on national lines for hundreds of years. Manufacturing, marketing and purchasing patterns were national in scope. The removal of regulatory barriers does not in itself create a true single market overnight. The establishment of a true common market in business terms with major cross-border distribution and marketing infrastructure occurs gradually. The Commission recognises and accepts this.

Once the market has been defined, the economic power of the merging firms can be assessed. This in itself is a two-stage analysis. Firstly market shares must be calculated. These are very important as an indication of market power. A large market share gives a firm a presence on the market that, sometimes in itself, will make it an unavoidable trading partner for its customers. In *Hoffman-La Roche versus Commission*, the Court observed: "The view may legitimately be taken that very large shares are in themselves, save in exceptional circumstances, evidence of the existence of a dominant position."[4] The Court went even further in its recent judgement in the AKZO case, holding that a firm with a 50% market share is per se dominant in the absence of exceptional circumstances.[5]

Thus, in some extreme cases, very high market shares can in themselves be sufficient to indicate dominance. However, in most cases, high market shares alone are insufficient to prove dominance as they represent only a snapshot of the market. In the Hoffman-La Roche case, for example, the Court confirmed the need to examine the ability of an allegedly dominant firm to maintain high market shares over time before dominance could be established. It is therefore

---

4. Hoffman-La Roche versus Commission. Case 85/76. Judgement of 13 February 1979. ECR (1979) 461, at ground 41.

5. AKZO Chemie versus Commission. Case C-62/86. Judgement of 3 July 1991, not yet reported, at ground 60.

necessary to examine a number of other factors, of which the most important is whether actual and potential competition is sufficiently strong to prevent the merging firms from acting independently. Thus, a close examination of the size and competitive importance of rival firms remaining on the relevant market is necessary. For example, for MBB and Aérospatiale, the Commission was able to accept a merger in the civilian helicopter sector which would give high market shares to these two firms, because US manufacturers such as Sikorsky and Bell would act as real and effective competitors, preventing the new firm from acting independently. The American producers would in fact be particularly effective constraints on the merged company because of their high overall helicopter turnover due largely to US military orders.

Furthermore, markets are dynamic, and the Commission's analysis reflects this. An examination of the likelihood of entry is central to the Commission's approach. Entry barriers are therefore appraised, to determine whether there is a real likelihood of new entry. The basic question to be answered is whether the threat of new entry, in either product or geographical terms, will impose the necessary market discipline on the alleged dominant firm. In order to do so, entry must be possible and likely to occur within a short period of time following an increase in demand. A number of different entry barriers have already been identified in the decisions adopted under the Regulation. For example, in the proposed Alcatel/Telettra merger, the important role played by national regulation in restricting trade in the telecommunications sector was highlighted. In assessing potential entry, the Commission attempts a realistic examination of the market, analysing such factors as likely available demand to a new entrant, risk levels and technical entry difficulties, to establish whether entry is likely. The thirteenth report on competition sets out a series of factors relevant to this analysis.

In the light of all these factors, the Commission will conclude whether or not a notified concentration will give the merging firms that independence of action central to dominance. The Aérospatiale-Alenia/De Havilland case is a good example of how these numerous factors come together to enable a clear conclusion to be reached in a difficult and complicated case. It also provides a good example of how the Commission deals with a case from the procedural viewpoint.

Aérospatiale and Alenia operated a joint venture, ATR. This company was the world's leading regional turbo-prop aircraft manufacturer. ATR's parent firms sought to acquire De Havilland, the world number two, from Boeing. The Commission's investigation process began five months before notification, when it first became aware of the proposed agreement. During this period, all existing knowledge of regional aircraft manufacturing within the Commission - within DG-III and DG-IV in particular - was pooled and assessed. Discussions were held with Aérospatiale and Alenia as to the information to be provided in the notification.

As soon as the notification was received, the external inquiry was launched. Written questionnaires were immediately sent to all the competitors, to all the potential competitors such as jet aircraft manufacturers, and to a very large number of customers worldwide. Together with the information obtained from Aérospatiale and Alenia, the answers enabled the Commission to determine the geographical reference market and relevant product markets. It was relatively easy to establish that the geographical reference market was the world. There are no tangible barriers to the import of aircraft into the EC, and, almost by definition, there are negligible transport costs. There is also significant market penetration, in particular between the markets of North America and Europe.

Establishing the relevant product markets was slightly more difficult. There was general consensus within the aircraft industry and amongst airlines that jet and turbo-prop aircraft did not fulfil the same functions. The Commission then spent much time and effort examining the question of whether turbo-prop regional aircraft constitute a single relevant product market, or require subdivision into categories. The vast majority of the industry, both manufacturers and purchasers, divide the sector into aircraft with 20-39 seats, 40-59 seats and 60 or more seats. The aeroplanes in these different categories are fundamentally different as regards their characteristics, price and intended use. A 30-seat plane costs approximately half the price of a 60-seat one. In the light of these various factors, the degree of substitutability between planes in the three categories cannot by any stretch of the imagination be considered substantial. It should not be forgotten that airlines lease or purchase planes to fit the distance and expected passenger turnover for the route in question, not vice versa. This conclusion was almost universally supported on both sides of the industry. In this light, the Commission's approach to market definition can hardly be considered to be some sort of legalistic application of doctrinaire policy.

Regarding market shares, in the 40-59 segment the merged firm would have had considerably in excess of 50% of the world market. Even if the various segments of the regional turbo-prop aircraft market were considered together, the merged group would still have had in excess of 50% of the world market. These market shares put the operation in the Court of Justice's category of operations that in normal circumstances result in per se dominance. Nonetheless, the Commission undertook a very detailed examination of both remaining actual competition and potential entry, which in the final analysis was the most fundamental aspect of the case.

The remaining manufacturers were either small in resource terms compared with ATR and De Havilland combined, or had relatively few turbo-prop activities and limited product ranges. There was general consensus within the industry that the markets were approaching maturity. Potential entry on a significant scale was considered extremely unlikely; market exit, in fact, was felt to be more plausible. All available data supported these views.

In the light of these facts, the finding of dominance and a significant impediment to competition was inevitable. This finding was supported by nine of the eleven Member States present in the Advisory Committees. I am convinced that no other responsible competition authority could have reached a different conclusion on the facts before it.

I remarked earlier that there is no conflict between Community industrial and competition policies. I believe that, with mature reflection, the De Havilland decision will be seen clearly to reflect this fact. The European turbo-prop aircraft industry is already leading the world. With competitive markets assured, I predict that we shall see it prosper for many years to come.

The De Havilland case, like all the cases dealt with by the Commission to date, concerned single-firm dominance. The gradual market integration within the Community is continual and inevitable. For example, there can be no doubt that in time the starter-battery market - considered national in the CEAC/Magneti-Marelli case - will become a Community market. As this process continues, a basic question must be addressed. Are we willing to accept the development of Community markets, through merger and acquisition, in which only a handful of companies compete? In some world markets, where companies must have a minimum size to be efficient and competitive, this is inevitable. Such cases are not, however, of concern in this respect. The pressure from firms outside the EC will ensure these companies remain competitive. The problem I wish to raise concerns markets where no such minimum efficient scale of operation exists.

Where only a limited number of firms remain in such a market, oligopolistic structures can develop. In such circumstances firms may find themselves consciously or unconsciously following the prices of their few competitors. This can quickly result in higher prices for the consumer, and restricted innovation and progress. Many economists argue that a bad oligopoly can be even worse than a sole dominant position. A dominant position of a single firm can often erode over time. The erosion process can be difficult and costly for the consumer, but it may still occur. A strong oligopoly in a mature market with higher entry barriers can last a lifetime.

Article 2(1) highlights the Regulation's fundamental aim: "to maintain and develop effective competition within the common market". It is my belief that the concept of dominance in Article 2 of the Regulation covers oligopolistic dominance. If a merger or acquisition creates or reinforces a market structure on which price collusion or price parallelism between companies is highly likely, that concentration should be considered incompatible with the common market.

This view is not new. The structural control of oligopoly constitutes one of the basic aims of US merger control and exists in the relevant United Kingdom and German legislation. Although the detailed circumstances necessary for a finding of oligopolistic dominance will have to be developed through case-law, in can be stated that two factors in particular will need to be present. First, there will be a limited number of large players on the market; a large number of market participants of varying sizes makes collusion or price parallelism difficult or impossible. Second, the market is likely to be mature, with high entry barriers; in markets where new entrants are likely, or innovation and change play a key role, collusion or price parallelism are not usually present.

It is only a question of time before the first case of oligopolistic dominance has to be dealt with by the Commission. As the single-market process produces results in terms of truly integrated markets from the business point of view, the control of oligopolies can be expected to play a central role in the Commission's continuing policy of creating a true and competitive common market.

Our initial implementation of merger control at the Community level has been widely, if not universally, regarded as successful. There remains much work to be done. We must further refine our analytical and investigative skills, and attempt to make our decision-making process as transparent and predictable as possible. Nonetheless, I believe that our early experience indicates that the Regulation provides a rational, effective and viable procedure for continuing to develop Community-wide merger control in the long term.

4. The internal market

It has become trite to say that the internal market is a process rather than a date. Of course, there is some truth in this, but we must not lose sight of our common commitment in the Community to the creation of a single market without internal frontiers by the end of 1992. Since 1985 the EC has been engaged in a remarkable exercise: the creation of a single barrier-free market out of 12 separate national markets. There is still a lot of work to do and 1992 will be a very busy year for the Community institutions.

First, we have not done enough in the area of taxation and company law. It is still easier for a company to have two plants in the same country than one in two different countries. The Commission has done its job in putting forward proposals, but Ministers are still hesitating.

Second, everyone agrees that common standards will make it easier for companies to exploit the economies of scale of the single market, but progress towards European standardisation is painfully slow, again because of bickering over narrow points of national interest.

Third, public procurement markets are supposed to be opened up to competition, but the Commission regularly has to intervene in cases where the agreed rules are not being followed.

Fourth, as we get closer to an integrated market, the pressures of competition will increase, as will the temptation for governments to give a little help to "their" companies or for companies themselves to engage in restrictive practices so as to steal a march on their competitors. The Commission will have to be increasingly vigilant in order to ensure that competition in the single market is fair and takes place on the basis of comparative advantage rather than access to public funds or the ability to squeeze out competition.

Competition policy in the past

Over the years, competition policy has been applied to encourage - sometimes to force - companies and consumers to treat the Community as one market when making their commercial decisions. We were frequently accused of putting the cart before the horse - or, as the lawyers would put it, using a legal fiction - when we told companies to organise their distribution systems on the basis that consumers in the Community should be able to buy goods in any of its Member States under the conditions prevailing there. We were told to wait until the common market, as we called it then, really existed before asking companies to plan their activities on that basis.

I am sure that we were right not to heed those criticisms. If European industry was one of the earliest and most fervent and consistent supporters of the internal market programme, it is in some part due to the fact that companies had become used to thinking in single-market terms from the beginning of the application of competition policy in the 1960's.

The impact of the internal market on competition policy

Now that the internal market is nearly a reality in many sectors of the economy, it is time to consider what approach competition policy should adopt when it is achieved.

The first impact of the internal market on policy arises because a prerequisite for competition policy analysis is the definition of the relevant geographical market. One cannot know the effect of a particular transaction on competition unless one knows where that competition is actually taking place. Our experience in applying the merger regulation so far shows that there are already many Community-wide markets, and others in transition from national to Community status. Indeed, some are worldwide, such as those for civilian helicopters and commuter aircraft. On the other hand, some remain national, regional or even local because of transport costs or other inelasticities. In the service industries, some markets tend to be and will remain local in nature. In all these cases, we have to look carefully at the barriers to entry which might still be separating geographical markets within the Community or between the Community and the rest of the world. The internal market process is certainly extending the size of many industrial markets, and the Commission of course welcomes this development. Competition policy carries out a dynamic analysis of market realities and takes account of the foreseeable consequences of the internal market process within a reasonable time-scale. But in this area we have to engage in an objective analysis of what the market is or is about to become, not what we would like it to be.

The second impact of the internal market is on the Commission's approach to getting the best out of European industry. The internal market creates enormous new opportunities for the Community's companies and consumers. Including the EFTA countries in our European Economic Area, we have 380 million consumers. The companies which will prosper in our internal market will be those capable of meeting the challenge posed by the elimination of barriers between Member States. Consumers are no longer captive in their own country and there will be competition for their custom from all over the Community. There will be a downward pressure on costs and prices and an upward pressure on efficiency and performance. Companies are reacting to this challenge in many ways. Some choose to go it alone and perfect the skills, resources and advantages they already have. Some will combine their forces through mergers, joint ventures and other co-operative alliances. The role of competition policy in a mature system is to facilitate this process and to step in only where competition is threatened. The restructuring of many European industries is already under way, and my job is to ensure that the playing-field remains level and that the benefits are passed on in the form of consumer satisfaction and industrial competitiveness.

I am frequently asked whether the Commission and other Community institutions should intervene in this restructuring process with an "industrial policy". My answer is that the right approach is the one that we have been following. This involves the continued deregulation and integration of the single market, in combination with the implementation of competition policy. It is backed up with the considered use of schemes to encourage regional development, progress in technical research and development, training and the advancement of small and medium-sized enterprises. We should not go further by tinkering with specific sectors and companies, whether by choosing and building up national or European champions or by propping up ailing concerns. In each of these areas, assistance should be as "horizontal" as possible, in the sense that it should give all qualifying companies an equal opportunity to take advantage of the aid.

Some companies will understandably be worried about the uncertainties which the internal market brings. The endeavour to build a Community market with competitive conditions resembling those of national markets is part of the effort to encourage companies to extend their activities into new areas. One danger I see in the reaction of the worried company is the idea that it can seek a defensive retrenchment in cartels and other anti-competitive practices. Here of course, competition policy will intervene promptly to stop any attempt to re-erect barriers between our Member States and to deny the benefits of the internal market to the consumer. Competition policy is at the service of industry and consumers alike and the well-advised company seeks informal guidance from DG-IV before embarking on any venture which might bring it into conflict with the Community's competition law.

Competition policy is not only a matter of concern for companies. Governments too have to take it into consideration when planning their strategies and activities in the internal market. In the state-aid field, a subsidy for one company is usually a competitive disadvantage for another which does not enjoy the generous support of the taxpayer. The internal market also seeks to promote cohesion between the various countries and regions of the Community. Considerable effort and a good deal of money are devoted by the Community to the development of its less-developed regions. Competition policy plays its part in this process by making sure that the Ministers of Finance in the richer, central regions of the Community do not undo or undermine the cohesion efforts being made elsewhere. More generally, subsidies could become the last resort of the protectionists within the Community, and competition policy has the difficult and important task of vigilance and, where necessary, sanction in this context. The Commission said in its 20th Competition Policy Report earlier this year that: "A reinforced state-aid policy is not only vital to the successful completion of the internal market, but a necessary prerequisite if the projected gains from such integration are to be realised." This does not mean that all state aid is or will be forbidden. Rather, it should be concentrated on purposes and in areas where it is most needed.

An important issue thrown up by the internal market process has been the growing realisation that many important sectors of industry are linked in ways not always evident to policy-makers in Brussels. For example, the strengthening of the telecommunications and information-technology industries requires the release of pent-up demand which the absence of a genuine internal market has stifled. This means that procurement must be opened up and liberalisation pursued to introduce competition in the industries which use telecommunications and information technology, to an extent consistent with the maintenance of certain public-service obligations. But it goes further than the liberalisation of telecommunications. For example, I have been struck in my dual capacity as Commissioner responsible for competition policy and financial institutions by the fact that the opening-up of financial-service markets in the Community is essential for the well-being of telecommunications equipment and computer producers. This is only one example. We have encouraged companies to "think European" and they have begun to plan their activities on that basis. We would be letting them down and failing in our internal-market ambitions if we allowed demand to remain constrained behind national barriers. Those barriers are no longer the physical ones represented by customs officials at the border. Barriers to trade are much more subtle today. They involve dominant positions, standardisation issues, exclusive rights, procurement practices and subsidies. In the internal market, it is the role of competition policy to prise open markets which are still blocked and to make sure, once they are open, that they remain so.

I therefore believe that the coming years will see a considerable degree of enforcement of competition policy in traditionally highly-regulated industries. I know that Article 90 of the Treaty of Rome has been controversial among lawyers and politicians, but it is clear to me on analysis of what is really needed in the Community that it is a very necessary instrument indeed. The foresight of the authors of the Treaty in 1957 should once again be applauded. Striking the balance between liberalisation and public-service requirements is never easy, but it is right in the Community that the Commission be given that task. The Commission will of course carry out wide-ranging consultations in applying Article 90 and I would expect it to have the full support of those who want a genuine internal market.

The completion of the internal market will also have an impact on the day-to-day application of competition policy by the Commission. Under Articles 85 and 86, the Commission has jurisdiction when there is an "effect on trade between Member States". This may be direct or indirect, actual or potential, but it must exist. If there is no such effect on trade, the matter is one for the Member States and not for the Commission. This rule has been in the Treaty from the very beginning and has given rise to a considerable body of practice and case law. Now in the internal market one would expect many more commercial transactions to have an effect on trade between Member States. Some have suggested that this will lead to a Commission takeover of competition policy for the whole Community, with the national competition authorities playing a very reduced, subsidiary role. Let me make it clear that this is not my ambition. In fact, the internal market has already set in motion certain trends which point in the opposite direction. We have been trying for some time to decentralise the application of our competition law by encouraging private actions in the national courts. I must admit that we have not been very successful so far, but we will be bringing forward new ideas soon which should give this process a boost. The Court of Justice has given added impetus to this development in its recent Delimitis judgment. As envisaged by the Court, the Commission stands ready to assist national judges in determining matters of Community competition law and will act as a genuine *amicus curiae* in doing so.

Another important development relevant to this approach is the unanimous decision taken by the Member States in the Council to adopt the Community merger-control regulation on the basis of a division of jurisdiction between the Commission and the national competition authorities. This marks a major departure from the system of concurrent jurisdiction prevailing under Articles 85 and 86. While I do not expect this to happen overnight, I would not be surprised if over the coming years the notion of effect on trade between Member States is given a more flexible interpretation by the Commission and the Courts in order to allow the national courts to deal with many more matters of principally national scope, leaving the Commission to deal with the larger, transnational or Community-wide transactions.

One might well ask whether this is possible or indeed desirable, when national and Community laws and procedures are so different. In other words, is the single regulatory-control principle compatible with a level playing-field? I do not, however, think the situation is as bleak as some would suggest. Without any attempt by the Commission to propose harmonisation of national competition laws and procedures, which some have argued would be the best solution but which would certainly be a lengthy and arduous task, we have seen over the last few years a growing convergence of national competition regimes with the Community's law and practice. Some have described this as a process of "soft" or voluntary harmonisation. We are still a long way from pure harmony, but in an increasing number of Member States competition laws have been passed which resemble what we have been doing in the Community for these last 30 years. My own country has not been in the forefront of this process, although the British Government's intentions as expressed in a White Paper are entirely praiseworthy. The spirit is willing, but apparently the Parliamentary time is lacking. In Belgium, on the other hand, the new competition law seems to me a fine example of national legislation designed to dovetail with Community law. Another fine example of recent legislation is Italy, where the new competition authority has already begun work in an impressive manner.

Some commentators have pointed to the boom in national competition legislation as an ironic consequence of the single regulatory-control system introduced by the Community merger-control regulation. I must say that I do not see any irony here. The Commission is delighted that Member States are taking their own responsibilities for competition policy seriously, and the only reservation we have is that the thresholds which divide our jurisdiction over

mergers from theirs are set too high. In the internal market, the Community and
the Member States share the common duty of ensuring, in the words of Article
3(f) of the Treaty of Rome, that a "system of undistorted competition" is
created. Our consumers and companies need nothing less and, as long as the job
is done effectively, do not really mind who does it. The Commission's
particular skills and responsibilities cover the transnational arrangements which
require an analysis of the Community economy as a whole and the gathering of
facts from several countries. I think that that is the Commission's real
responsibility and one which it has discharged well these last 30 years.

My final point on the impact of the completion of the internal market on
competition policy concerns our relations with the rest of the world. More and
more, our trading partners in the US, Japan and elsewhere look to the
Commission for a dialogue on the growing importance of competition policy for
the preservation and development of the world trading system. The Commission
has recently concluded an agreement with the United States of America
regarding co-operation and co-ordination in the field of competition policy. The
Commission also maintains a constant dialogue with the competition authorities
of many non-EC countries in order to help ensure that competitive principles are
respected world-wide. Just as traditional protectionism is a policy of the past
within the European Community, there is a growing realisation that it is not
enough to dismantle tariff barriers and retrain custom officials for other
activities in order to sustain the principles of free trade throughout the world.
The problems we have faced in the Community of dominant positions,
restrictive distribution systems, procurement practices, subsidies and exclusive
or monopoly rights confront us again when we step outside our borders into the
wider world. If the problems are similar, it is likely that the solutions will not be
very different either. The Commission has some experience of prising open
markets and creating level playing-fields. I expect competition policy to play an
important part in the coming years in international affairs. We expect our major
trading partners to apply their competition policies vigorously and without
discrimination in order to ensure that competitive opportunities within their
territories are open to all. This is a theme to which I return constantly when
talking to American, Japanese and other ministers and businessmen.

Conclusion

Competition policy has played an important part in bringing us to the verge of
completion of the internal market. The internal market, in turn, poses new
challenges for competition policy which will involve a shift of focus from the
Member-State to the Community level and beyond. I believe that the
Community has the necessary experience to meet this challenge successfully.

5. Financial services

While the Community's competition rules apply in the same way to all sectors of the economy, it is necessary for the Commission to take full account of the characteristics of particular industries when developing competition policy and enforcing its rules - and this is particularly true in the case of financial services.

One factor of which account must be taken is the nature and extent of the specific regulatory controls to which banks, insurance companies and other financial institutions are subject. Regulation is not a substitute for competition, but a framework for it. Competition is particularly important in highly-regulated industries, if companies are to satisfy the demands of consumers in the Community's single market and ensure their own long-term success. Where regulation is necessary to safeguard investor, depositor or consumer welfare, competition policy should complement it by ensuring that once the relevant standards have been met, genuine competition prevails in the market concerned.

Financial services are of major importance economically - now accounting for some 8% of Community GNP. They have grown enormously in the last decade and are increasingly international; it is estimated that the savings to be gained from the removal of technical barriers in this field amount to 20bn ECU. Some 80% of banking services are used by other firms outside the sector in the course of their business, so banking is the oil which lubricates the wheels of trade within the Community and between the Community and the rest of the world. Insurance and other financial services play a similar role in domestic and international transactions.

I will consider first how Articles 85 and 86 have been applied to the financial services sector, then I will go on to discuss our recent experience of the Merger Regulation in relation to the sector.

Articles 85 and 86

Article 85 prohibits agreements or understandings between firms or decisions of associations of firms which affect trade between Member States and have as their object or effect the prevention, restriction or distortion of competition within the Common Market. Such agreements are legally void and unenforceable. Parties which have been aggrieved by the effects of such arrangements may seek damages in national courts or bring complaints to the Commission. However, some agreements with redeeming economic, technical and consumer benefits may be exempted from this prohibition by the Commission. A further prohibition is found in Article 86 of the EEC Treaty which prohibits abusive behaviour by dominant firms. Such abuses can take the form of excessive or discriminatory pricing or the collective boycotting of a smaller competitor. The existence of a dominant position as such is not banned, only its exploitation or abuse. Fines of up to 10% of the turnover of the firms involved can be imposed by the Commission where it finds that these rules have been infringed.

How have these rules been applied to the financial services sector up to now? How should they be applied in the future? Before 1981, it was argued on behalf of many banking associations and their members that the financial sector enjoyed a general exemption from the competition rules by virtue of Article 90(2) of the EEC Treaty. Under this provision, firms entrusted with the operation of services of general economic interest are excluded from the normal competition regime of Articles 85-90. Needless to say, the Commission consistently opposed this view. The Court of Justice supported the Commission in the important Zuchner judgment of 1981.[1]

The Commission has always considered that the competition rules apply to all financial institutions. The provisions of Article 85(3), which allow for exemptions from the normal prohibition of restrictive agreements and practices, together with those of Article 90(2) which relate to public-service requirements, are quite sufficient to cater for the specific needs of such institutions.

Banking

One of the most important decisions taken by the Commission in the banking field, and one which best illustrates Commission policy, is the Eurocheques decision adopted in 1984. The Eurocheque payment system was created by a number of European financial institutions. The aim was to meet the growing need for international payment systems resulting from the growth of tourism and business travel within Europe, by making available a means of payment for use both at home and abroad. The system is based on the principle that the issuing banks supply the guarantee card and the cheques and that the format and design of these cheques are the same across Europe; the accepting banks are for their part obliged to pay these guaranteed cheques. In establishing this international payment system, member banks agreed on certain standard conditions, including (a) that a maximum inter-bank commission of 1.25% of the cheque amount could be charged; and (b) that a maximum amount of 170 ECU would be guaranteed under the system.

These two conditions restricted competition and were caught by Article 85(1). However, the Commission was prepared to grant an exemption because the system as a whole produced considerable consumer and economic benefits and because the two restrictions were not unreasonable or excessive. While the Commission was prepared to accept a measure of standardisation in the system, it imposed the condition, as the price of this acceptance, that the banks inform their customers in detail of the charges and deductions being made for the issuing and accepting of a Eurocheque.

---

1. Case 172/80, 1981 ECR 2021.

In this decision, the Commission drew an important distinction between inter-bank and bank-client relations - a distinction which it has continued to make ever since. Certain restrictions of competition may be tolerated between banks because of the efficiencies they produce, provided that there is no adverse impact on bank-client relations, which must remain subject to competition. The Commission found in the Eurocheques case that the multilateral inter-bank agreement about the level of inter-bank commission to be paid for the processing of Eurocheques could be exempted under Article 85(3). This was the first time the Commission had exempted a price-fixing agreement. It was exempted in this case on the basis that the multilateral agreement only established a maximum commission, so that there was still room for competition below this level.

However, the Commission took the view that inter-bank co-operation should not extend to relations with customers. Each bank must remain free to determine independently the price and terms of its customer services. As mentioned earlier, the decision expressly required the issuing bank to furnish details to its clients of the charges deducted for Eurocheque transactions. In particular it must make clear the exchange rate, the commission received by the accepting bank and any further charges imposed by the central clearing system or the issuing bank.

The exemption granted by the Commission in 1984 expired in 1986. A formal extension has not been granted. This is because the level of compliance with the exemption conditions has not always been satisfactory. The Commission has also been concerned to ensure that the maximum amount cleared within the Eurocheque system should be increased to allow Eurocheques to play their part in developing payment systems for the EC's internal market. A final problem is that the principal French banks have been charging retailers a commission for processing Eurocheques. This commission is the same as for credit cards. It results from an agreement made between the French banks represented by the Groupement des Cartes Bancaires and Eurocheque. The effect of this agreement has been to reduce the acceptability of Eurocheques in France and to provide French banks with two commissions for the same transaction. These problems are currently the subject of formal legal proceedings under Article 85(1). They do not detract from the significant benefits which the Eurocheque system has provided to consumers carrying out cross-frontier business, and I hope that satisfactory solutions to the problems can be found.

The Commission has confirmed the policy lines laid down in the Eurocheque decision in a series of cases concerning agreements notified by a number of national banking associations. The first of these concerned an agreement between the four main Irish banks on opening hours and on direct-debit and clearing systems. The Commission took the view that the arrangements on opening hours were not caught by Article 85(1), because the effect on competition was not sufficiently appreciable. The Direct-Debit and Clearing Rules were found to have no impact on competition whatsoever.

In 1986 the Commission exempted an agreement between Belgian banks on the maximum amount of inter-bank commission to be paid on certain transactions where one bank was acting as intermediary for the other. This agreement was exempted because it led to an improvement in services offered to clients. The amount was only a maximum and there was no obligation to pass the cost of this commission on to the customer.

The Italian banking association notified a series of 15 agreements to the Commission in 1984. Of these 15 notifications, five were abandoned at the request of the Commission; one was found to be of a technical nature only and not restrictive; while six others were found to be restrictive because they set the commissions and value dates for certain inter-bank transactions. However, it was felt that there was no appreciable affect on trade between Member States and so they were not caught by Article 85(1). The three remaining agreements related to the processing of cheques and bills and to a new system of uniform travellers' cheques and were found to be caught by Article 85(1) but worthy of exemption. They gave rise to rationalisation and standardisation producing greater efficiencies and lower costs. It is important to note that the banks remained free to decide how much or how little of the inter-bank commission would or could be charged to the client.

Another decision led to the abandonment by the Dutch banks of agreements on minimum commissions for services between banks and their clients and between banks themselves on uniform value dates, exchange rates and margins, and uniform commissions and exclusivity clauses for certain foreign-exchange brokers. The Commission, however, exempted a circular relating to the simplification of cheque-clearing procedures. In this case, the Commission confirmed its position on the need to distinguish between inter-bank relations and relations between a bank and its clients. In fact in this case, we sought the termination of both types of agreement, and not simply the bank-client type, because the inter-bank commission agreement was not found to be necessary for the proper functioning of the system. This case was also the first in which the Commission considered discriminatory bank commissions. Here the discrimination lay in the fact that a distinction was made between members of the Dutch Bankers' Association, foreign banks and non-members, and different commissions were charged for transfers between Dutch accounts and accounts outside the Netherlands.

Price cartels, whether in the form of agreements on commission levels, interest rates or interest-rate margins, are as reprehensible in this sector as in any other. The Commission's intervention led to the abandonment by several of the Community's national banking associations of agreements and recommendations on commission rates for various banking services. Such arrangements have few if any redeeming benefits - at any rate none for the consumer, who normally ends up paying more for a lower-quality service. Some national banking associations have argued that a degree of co-ordination of interest-rate levels was a necessary and legitimate objective of monetary policy. But there is no evidence that such co-ordination is necessary. It is perfectly possible for the monetary authorities to pursue and implement their own objectives of monetary policy without encouraging the use of illicit price cartels. Where such cartels are found to exist, the Commission will insist on their termination. The Commission's investigations are currently being carried out in each Member State. Already the Belgian banks have abandoned an agreement imposing a maximum interest rate of 0.5% for the remuneration of current accounts.

One issue which seems to arise with more than usual frequency in this sector is that of self-regulation. Often the self-regulation is carried out by the relevant trade association or by an exchange. In general, competition policy is neutral as regards self-regulation. There may be benefits to members in terms of increased flexibility and to the authorities in terms of lower costs. However, from a competition perspective our concern would be with the rules of the regulatory body. We would seek to ensure that, where membership of an association is important for access to or participation in a market, the rules governing admission comply with certain fundamental principles. The criteria for admission must be clear, precise and objective. Decisions on admission must be reasoned and subject to appeal within the association. The association should never prohibit members from using their right to appeal to the national courts. These principles have been applied in a series of decisions relating to various futures and commodity markets in London in the mid-1980's and more recently to the rules of the Association of International Bond Dealers which are still under consideration.

A further illustration of the above principles is provided by the Sarabex case. Under an arrangement between the British Bankers' Association and the Foreign Exchange and Currency Deposit Brokers' Association, banks were not permitted to use foreign-exchange brokers who were not members of the Brokers' Association, the rules of which also prohibited members from charging rates of commission differing from agreed rates. Following Commission intervention, the Bank of England introduced a more flexible system whereby banks could deal with brokers "recognised" by the Bank of England, such recognition being granted on the basis of objective criteria and subject to an appeal procedure under the Appeals Committee Chairman of the City Panel on Mergers and Takeovers. In addition, the recommended commission rates were changed to maxima.

Regarding savings banks, the Commission has recently set out its policy on co-operation agreements between these institutions following notification of some 30 such agreements. As mentioned earlier, we are not opposed to inter-bank arrangements which provide for greater rationalisation or standardisation and hence greater efficiency. For example, the multilateral agreement on the inter-operability of automatic teller machines would not normally cause competition problems. But the Commission has noted four particular problems which may cause difficulty. These are a) agreements between savings banks not to enter each other's geographical territory; b) agreements not to conclude similar arrangements with other credit institutions on a savings bank's territory; c) exclusiveness granted to certain banks in their home country for dealing in and distributing common products; and d) a priori control by a national association over bilateral agreements signed by its members.

This brief review has served to show that we are not opposed to co-operation between banks. Where such co-operation produces economic efficiencies which can be passed on to the consumer in the form of better service at a lower cost, we are all in favour. And of course if consumers are to avail themselves of this improved service or lower price, they must be made fully aware of the price they are paying and the service to which it applies. Information to the consumer, therefore, clarity and transparency are key concepts in this context. It is quite clear, however, that much co-operation does *not* benefit the consumer. A competitive internal market for all financial services is essential for industry and the private customer alike.

Insurance

Similar principles apply in the insurance sector. As with banking, the general applicability of the competition rules to insurance is beyond doubt. This was confirmed by the Court of Justice in the German Fire Insurance Case,[2] where the Commission had prohibited a recommendation made by the German Property Insurers' Association to its members to increase premiums by specified percentages on all policies. The Commission prohibited this recommendation on the grounds that it had as its very object the restriction of price competition between members of the association. We did not even need to demonstrate that members had actually applied the recommendation. Predictably, the German Association argued that there was no restrictive effect since members were free to apply the recommendation or not. Neither the Commission nor the Court accepted this argument.

We are now preparing a Block-Exemption Regulation in insurance which will create legal certainty and provide the industry with the necessary guidance on where the line between acceptable and unacceptable co-operation should be drawn. The Council granted the Commission the necessary enabling power to make such a Regulation in June 1991. Work on a first draft is well under way. The Council Regulation requires the Commission to publish a draft so that interested parties may comment.

The Council has specifically proposed the exemption of certain agreements in the following categories: a) the calculation of pure premium, i.e. the pure statistical cost of a given risk, excluding any element relating to overhead costs or profit; b) the drafting of standard policy conditions; c) the formation of reinsurance and co-insurance groupings; d) co-operation on procedures for claims settlement; e) co-operation in regard to research and the testing and use of security equipment; and f) the maintenance and exchange of information on aggravated risks.

Strict conditions will be attached to the exemption of co-operation agreements in order to ensure that we exempt only those which provide genuine economic and consumer benefits and which are really necessary to secure such benefits.

---

2. Case 45/85, VDS v. Commission.

The Merger Regulation

Finally, I would like to mention the application of the Merger Regulation to financial services. The principles underlying the Regulation apply to the financial-service sector in exactly the same way as to other sectors of the economy.

Of some 60 notifications under the Regulation since its entry into force on 21 September 1990, four have involved mergers between banks and three have involved insurance companies. Amongst these, Dresdner Bank and the Banque Nationale de Paris have created a common structure in Hungary and Czechoslovakia and two Japanese banks, Kyowa and Saitama, have merged.

Before looking at these cases, I shall outline the methodology of the Regulation in the financial-service context. I will not go into it in detail here, as I have devoted an earlier chapter to merger policy. But the nature of much financial business means that the general methodology is not always appropriate in this sector.

The first problem is that financial institutions have no "turnover" comparable to that of other firms. Most of the income of a credit institution normally results from interest received on loans and advances. It is therefore necessary to develop particular rules instead of the normal 5bn and 250m ECU turnover criteria, in order to apply the thresholds of the Regulation to this sector. Article 5(3) of the Regulation sets these out.

For banks and other financial institutions the aggregate worldwide turnover criterion - 5bn ECU aggregate turnover - is replaced by one-tenth of the total assets of the financial institutions concerned. The Community turnover criterion is replaced by multiplying one-tenth of total assets by the ratio between loans and advances to credit institutions and customers resident in the EC and total loans and advances. Similarly, turnover within a single Member State is calculated by multiplying one-tenth of total assets by the ratio between loans and advances to borrowers resident in that Member State and total loans and advances if that total turnover was generated within a single Member State. If this figure exceeds two-thirds of the EC-generated turnover figure, and this is true for all the firms concerned, then the thresholds would not be met.

The use of total assets and loans and advances was considered to be more representative of financial activity than other measures of banking output. There are nonetheless problems in ensuring both that these criteria produce a result broadly equivalent to that achieved in other sectors, and the same outcome for different types of financial institutions. Banks, for example, can create credit which appears on their balance sheet. There are certain other types of financial institution, such as companies principally involved in fund management, credit cards, securities trading or corporate financial advice, which are not in this position. Another difficulty is that the calculation of Community and national turnover might produce odd results where the credit activities of the financial institution in question represent a small proportion of its total assets. This might be the case in respect of certain holding companies. Further, the calculation of turnover within the Community requires banks and other financial institutions to distinguish financial operations according to the residence of their client.

In the light of all these factors, the Commission and the Council of Ministers have made clear that these provisions may be modified in the light of the comments of regulatory authorities and the market practitioners themselves. When the Regulation was adopted, the Council and Commission observed, in a note clarifying the scope of certain of its articles, that "the criterion defined as a proportion of assets should be replaced by a concept of banking income as referred to in Directive 86/635 on the annual accounts and consolidated accounts of banks and other financial institutions, either at the time of entry into force of the relevant provisions of that Directive, or at the time of the review of the thresholds."

This Directive defines banking income as the sum of interest-receivable and similar income, income from securities, commissions receivable, net profit on financial operations and other operating income. Thus, if the specific financial-turnover calculation is impossible or meaningless in a specific situation, an alternative has been identified. Turnover for insurance companies is calculated on the basis of income received from insurance premiums. In a mixed firm the turnover of the individual parts of a group is calculated individually according to the different rules and then added together.

The Regulation recognises that financial institutions may take a temporary shareholding in another company, for example through underwriting. Such holdings are not considered as potential mergers on three conditions: a) if the purchase has been made with a view to resale; b) if the shareholding rights are only exercised in order to prepare a sale; and c) if such holdings are sold in any case within one year. (The Commission can, however, extend this period if requested to do so by the purchasers and if it was not reasonably possible to arrange sale within one year.)

Equally, in the case of a pure investment operation, so long as voting rights are only used to maintain the value of investments and not to determine the competitive strategy of the firm, this too falls outside the terms of the Regulation. One recent example in this context concerned the syndicate of eight banks led by American Express which took over another company on the point of bankruptcy.[3] This was indeed considered to be a merger, essentially because the banks concerned did not intend to sell their shareholding within one year.

So far all decisions taken by the Commission in the banking sector have been decisions of approval: the mergers were cleared as being compatible with the common market. The Commission has judged that the firms concerned did not have a dominant position, in view of their small market share. Nonetheless, questions have been raised about the definition of a geographical market and how far it is meaningful to distinguish between different types of banking service to define a product market. The cases referred to us so far have not required us to refine our thinking in this area.

In the case of the Dresdner Bank/BNP joint venture, the Commission considered that the joint services to be offered in Hungary and Czechoslovakia

---

3. Kelt/American Express.

principally concerned those countries' own financial markets. As these were outside the Community there was no need for the Commission to consider what the effect on them would be. Equally, in certain international merger cases with repercussions for the banking market within the Community, the very small market share held by banks from outside the EC has allowed the Commission to keep open the question of whether Community banking markets are Community-wide or still to some extent national. In the Kyowa/Saitama case, the Commission left open the question of a precise definition of the service market in the banking sector, since even by the narrowest possible market definition, these banks' market shares remained negligible.

For the insurance sector the definition of product and geographical market has so far proved more straightforward. For example, in the UAP/Transatlantic case the Commission took the view that the relevant geographical market for life insurance was national while that for reinsurance was worldwide. The Commission also considered that distinct product markets existed for life insurance, reinsurance and each type of non-life insurance (fire, accident etc.). This confirmed the view taken in the AG/AMEV merger.

The fact that little jurisprudence has been established on questions of geographical or product market in the financial-service sector carries with it the advantage that the Commission is still able to take into account the experience of practitioners in particular markets. Our objective is to reinforce competition, not to enforce an arbitrary view of geographical or product markets. Nevertheless, it is clear that the question of market definition will in due course need to be looked at more closely.

In addition to the general criteria used in all sectors to define the relevant market, decisions in the financial-service sector will be particularly influenced by the move towards economic and monetary union in the Community. National markets limited by their own currency, and the often prohibitive costs of foreign-exchange dealing for small transactions, will simply disappear when a single European currency is introduced later in this decade.

No doubt national consumer preferences for particular financial services or types of saving instrument will continue to exist, though diminishing considerably over time. But the eminently-portable nature of most financial products means that EMU will transform retail financial-service markets, increasing competition in sectors hitherto sheltered from cross-border competition. This will be to the great benefit of the consumer, and over time to Europe's financial-service industry. And it will of course influence our assessment of the relevant market when considering merger cases.

Overall, then, the Merger Regulation provides a more transparent environment for mergers and acquisitions policy within the Community's internal market. Its application to the financial sector requires certain specificities to be taken into account; but it works on the same principles of ensuring fair and free competition as in other sectors.

The provision allowing particular prudential considerations to be taken into account in no way contradicts this basic principle. The Regulation provides a single regulatory-control procedure for competition issues. The question of whether the owners of a bank are fit and proper to do so, to use the English expression, is a separate issue to be decided by the appropriate supervisory authorities. It cannot be used as a disguised means of influencing the competitive aspects of a merger decision.

Conclusion

It must not be forgotten that the opening-up of the Community's financial-service markets is accompanied by a programme of legislation to provide for minimum standards and a single licence to do business throughout the EC. This legislation either has been adopted or is under discussion in the Council of Ministers. We are now in the final straight for the internal-market deadline of 1 January 1993.

The combination of competition policy enforcement, an open attitude towards external competition, and appropriate legislation at Community level will ensure that the single market has an efficient and successful financial-service sector. The Community's industries, its citizens and, last but not least, its financial institutions themselves have everything to gain from this process.

6. Transport

Until a few years ago, competition was largely absent from the transport industry, and even though the Commission was not short of ideas on the subject, the Member States and, I should say, the industry itself were unenthusiastic. This apparent neglect stands in sharp contrast to the importance of the industry. Personal travel accounts for about 15% of consumer spending in the Community and of an average of 2% of expenditure by business and government. Transport of merchandise accounts for a significant share of the costs of manufacturing industry. But the importance of transport goes beyond mere figures: these services are the lifeline of the Community's regions, providing the means to move people and goods to other regions and to the Community's central areas. Furthermore, transport services link the Community with the rest of the world. They are the vehicle for importing and exporting products and raw materials. Efficient transport therefore is a key component of cohesion within the Community and ties up the Community with the world economy.

Liberalisation

For a long time the transport sector was organised on the basis of regulation rather than competition. Governments intervened to regulate market access, capacity and prices, and industry organisations or international cartels added more restrictions - up to the point where, in air transport, IATA not only set prices but also became involved in deciding which and how much food could be given to passengers, and where, in shipping, "liner conferences" discussed with foreign governments whether outsiders should be given access to the trade. Not surprisingly, many Community markets were marked by monopoly or oligopoly supply, high prices and market-sharing; it may be doubted whether the Community's transport industry was as efficiently organised as it might have been and whether the Community transport user received a fair deal. Estimates of the gains in efficiency and cost savings from liberalisation vary, but for air transport in the Community recent research has suggested an amount of about 1.5bn ECU annually. No doubt similar gains could be expected for the other main modes of transport.

Fortunately, we are moving away from the antiquated, highly-regulated structure and most transport modes are now at least to some extent liberalised. Freedom of establishment and freedom to provide services are increasingly relevant to the transport industry: we have created, or are creating, market-access opportunities by enabling investment in carriers in a Member State by nationals of other Member States, and Member States cannot arbitrarily refuse licences to would-be carriers. Capacity restrictions are disappearing, and free

43

pricing is increasingly the norm rather than the exception.

However, 1993 is approaching fast, and in some sectors a lot of progress must still be made. We cannot expect to reap the full benefits of liberalisation in terms of high-quality services and low prices, until carriers have had to adapt to a genuinely open and competitive environment. Some bold steps have still to be taken: currently, for instance, the Council is discussing the Commission's proposals on the completion of the internal market in air transport, and there is no agreement yet on important subjects such as true freedom to provide services - the right of, say, Lufthansa to operate a service between Madrid and Rome, or between Paris and Nice.

Competition in transport

I like to think of liberalisation as creating scope for competition. That is probably why, as long as the Community had not formulated a liberalised transport policy, its competition policy was not applied in this sector. Indeed, when the Council in 1962 gave the Commission the power to implement the competition rules in the whole of the economy, it immediately removed transport from the scope of Regulation No. 17. The Commission only received powers to deal with anti-competitive practices in the transport industry at the same time as a transport policy was put into place - as happened in 1968 for inland transport (railways, inland waterways and road), in 1986 for shipping and in 1987 for air transport. However, there are still some gaps: the Commission has no power at present to apply the competition rules for instance to *cabotage* (maritime transport between ports of a single Member State), to tramp shipping, or to air transport within a Member State or to non-EC countries. The Commission has already made proposals to close these gaps for air transport, and proposals to do likewise in shipping will follow in due course.

In an industry which is in the process of liberalisation, the application of the competition rules is probably even more important than it is in others. The whole liberalisation effort, the relaxing of government restrictions on carriers, would have little effect if we were to allow carriers to re-introduce comparable restrictions by means of private action. The competition rules enable us to ensure that carriers do not prevent each other from making use of the opportunities created by liberalisation. For instance, when price controls are lifted, price-fixing cartels cannot be allowed to prevent the emergence of price competition. Government-imposed capacity limitations must not be replaced by market-sharing agreements. When market access is opened up, we must insist that new entrants are not denied the opportunity to use essential facilities or infrastructure such as airport slots or industry-wide computerised reservation systems.

One should also keep in mind that an industry emerging from a long period of regulation is usually dominated by a few oligopolists. Most Member States have for many decades organised their air-transport policies as a function of the needs of their flag carrier, with the result that these normally have a dominant position on their home markets. Hence there is a need for strict vigilance in order to avoid abuses of those dominant positions, in particular where dominance would be used to prevent the development of competition. For instance, the Commission intervened under Article 86 to oblige a dominant airline to grant access to its reservation system to a new competitor. The Commission is also considering the case of a dominant airline's refusal to share routes with a competitor, contrary to industry practice - an action which has the effect of making market access more difficult for the competitor. Consequently, the Commission may have to insist that dominant carriers relinquish some advantages they have inherited from regulation. For example, we allowed Air France to merge with UTA and Air Inter only on condition that route licences and slots were made available to competitors. The move from regulation to competition will be successful only if there are competitors able to take advantage of new opportunities.

Fortunately we *can* look forward to a more competitive environment in the medium term. Liberalisation will open up the dominant carriers' home bases to competition, so that the dominant positions which now exist may be eroded in the next few years.

Government intervention in a liberalised market

Where market-access opportunities are created and competition can develop, we also need to ensure that the playing-field is level and that governments do not intervene to distort competition in favour of some carriers. While state ownership in itself is perfectly compatible with the competition rules, Article 90 makes it clear that public companies, and companies to which Member States grant special or exclusive rights, are subject to the competition rules. Furthermore, there must be sufficient transparency as to the effects of state ownership. Finally, the Commission has a well-developed policy on state aid, and even though it is not my department which is responsible for monitoring state aid in the transport sector, the same rules apply as in other industries. That means that Member States must refrain from granting aid which distorts competition, that financial support must have a legitimate objective and that the amount of the support must be proportionate to the objective to be achieved. It is obvious that some of the particular features of the transport industry (public-service obligations, funding the cost of infrastructure, the need to restructure in order to adapt carriers to a more competitive environment) may mean that public funding is justified, but it is also obvious that state aid can cause serious distortions of competition, not only between different modes of transport but also between direct competitors, who will be penetrating each other's home bases much more frequently than in the past.

Restructuring the industry

I have already mentioned the fact that liberalisation is leading to a restructuring of the transport industry. So long as carriers are not exposed to effective competition, they can survive even if they are handicapped by inefficient structures and organisations. But competition is merciless in exposing these weaknesses; when users can choose between competing suppliers, they will show their preferences by deserting the carriers which cannot offer the low prices, the high quality or the wide range of services which their competitors are offering.

We are therefore already witnessing the widespread phenomenon - in particular in air transport and shipping - of carriers breaking out of their traditional and narrow home bases, constructing rational networks, pursuing economies of scale and of density and improving their financial bases. No doubt this movement will entail a consolidation of the industry and a reduction of the number of suppliers. There are many aspects of the restructuring movement which I welcome. If it improves the efficiency of the European transport industry, Community carriers will become more competitive worldwide, and transport users in the Community will have a wider choice between better and cheaper carriers.

That, I believe, is one of the main lessons we can learn from the deregulation of air transport in the United States: overall, fewer airlines can compete more intensely in a liberalised environment than a larger number of airlines in a regulated environment. But the American experience does not provide an acceptable model for Europe. From a competition perspective it gives rise to concern on two grounds.

First, even if competition at the level of the Community as a whole were to increase, one must avoid concentrations which give rise to monopolies or dominant positions in respect of substantial markets. Competition policy must be concerned about the domination by an airline of a particular airport, for instance, or of a route of significant size. Neither the consumer nor the airline will benefit from monopolies. We simply cannot tolerate, and the Treaty would not allow us to accept, that the European transport user should pay the price of the elusive pursuit of worldwide competitiveness.

Second, there must be a level of concentration which cannot be exceeded with impunity. In a tight oligopoly, the risk of collusion is real and there is no guarantee that competition between the few remaining carriers would be effective. In addition, even if there were genuine competition overall, there would probably be more individual markets in which effective competition was jeopardised than we could confidently handle by imposing safeguards to protect competition in specific situations. Therefore I favour the prevention of excessive concentration.

Other Commission initiatives

This brings me to the Commission's agenda for the application of the competition rules in the transport sector. In the field of inland transport, we are now concentrating on combined transport (rail/road), a mode of growing importance which in many instances provides for more efficient, yet flexible and environmentally-friendly long-haul transport. However, we must make sure that this mode develops into a competitive form of transport in the context of a single internal market, operating without market-sharing arrangements and with maximum price competition.

The shipping industry benefits from a very broad block-exemption regulation in favour of liner conferences. I do not believe the time is ripe for a reassessment of that exemption, but it should not be assumed that it will remain in force indefinitely. Meanwhile, we insist on the strict respect of the obligations attached to the block exemption, and we are considering sanctions against the West African liner conferences which took unacceptable measures to exclude outsiders from their trade. The Commission is also preparing a block exemption in favour of consortia agreements, under conditions which would provide for consultations between consortia and users and maintain effective competition within the consortia and with outsiders.

Finally, the air-transport sector has a busy agenda. I have already mentioned the need to reflect on the conditions under which restructuring operations would be allowed, and it is likely that the Commission will soon have the opportunity of putting those conditions into practice. Meanwhile, the third and final phase of liberalisation is being prepared and will include new block exemptions. These will be based on the existing ones, with the addition of an exemption in favour of joint operations on new air services. We are looking critically at the exemption in favour of tariff consultations between airlines, and are reflecting on the possibility of increasing price competition without jeopardising interlining relationships between airlines. Discussions between airlines in order to allocate slots at congested airports will continue to benefit from an exemption, provided sufficient safeguards exist - either in the block exemption, or in the common rules which the Council is considering - for new entrants to obtain slots at attractive times of the day. Finally, we will increasingly be looking at air services between the Community and non-EC countries. The Commission made a proposal a few years ago - which the Council still has on the table - to extend its powers into that area; meanwhile the issue needs to be addressed in the context of the air-transport agreement with Norway and Sweden and of the European Economic Area agreement, and in the framework of close relations with countries such as the United States, with which we have a special agreement on co-operation and the co-ordination of anti-trust enforcement activities.

Conclusion

I believe the Commission has lived up to the challenge of developing an internal market in transport. Much progress has been made in this sector in a short timespan, both in order to liberalise the different modes of transport and in order to instil the discipline of competition into the industry. The next few years will pose new problems, as the Community's industry restructures itself and adapts to the more competitive environment and as the European transport user begins to experience the concrete benefits of this new environment. On our part, considerable vigilance will be required in order to maintain the degree of competition without which liberalisation would just be an achievement on paper.

7. The Community's external relations

Since the second world war, and especially during the 1970's and 80's, companies have increasingly been operating across national borders. Until as recently as the beginning of the present Commission, the main issue, if not the only one, at the nexus of competition policy and international relations was the question of "extraterritoriality". How far could the arm of competition law stretch in apprehending the actions of foreign companies operating across or even beyond one's borders, with effects on competition within them? Much of the focus of this debate was on the perceived excessive exercise of competition jurisdiction by the Federal anti-trust authorities in the United States, illustrated by the adoption of blocking statutes by several of our Member States. No doubt the high point of this debate, which at times reached the proportions of a dispute, was marked, and epitomised, by the Laker Airways saga of measure and counter-measure across the Atlantic. The forward thinking of the present international anti-trust agenda could hardly be more distant from this *chacun chez soi* approach of a short time ago.

This does not mean that the scope of international jurisdiction is no longer an issue. But it is now recognised that whatever the precise jurisdictional tests applied, the international economic facts of life mean that there are bound to be substantial overlaps of competition jurisdiction. The process of globalisation of the world economy continues apace, as companies increasingly operate, not only across borders through trade, but also by establishing their own research, production and distribution facilities in many countries. The effects of their business decisions are liable to be felt in more than one jurisdiction, and often in several, each of which is liable to have grounds for reviewing those activities. And in order to review them, the authorities increasingly need to obtain information from outside their territory. The emphasis of the jurisdictional question is therefore shifting to the resolution or, better still, the avoidance of conflicts which may arise from the existence of such concurrent jurisdiction. At the same time, a perhaps more serious problem arising at this moment from the internationalisation of the world economy is the situation where certain important trading countries do not adequately enforce their competition rules, thereby leading to "negative" conflicts. I shall return to this in a moment.

The possibility of conflict arising as a result of concurrent enforcement activities between the Commission and the competition authorities of its main partners in international trade and investment was considerably increased as a result of the long-awaited adoption by the Council of a Regulation calling for the prior notification and vetting of large mergers of "Community dimension" by the Commission. And of course I should not omit to mention the Court's Woodpulp decision, which endorsed at least a qualified version of the "effects" doctrine of jurisdiction in 1988. Regarding agreements between North

American and Scandinavian producers to fix prices for the supply of woodpulp to buyers in the Community, the Court ruled that the Community had jurisdiction, on the basis that the price agreements were implemented in the Community through sales made to Community buyers.

At the same time, the Commission has been acting decisively over the last few years to bring the benefits of competition to many sectors in which it has been conspicuously lacking as a result of government-sponsored monopolies and restrictive practices. In so doing the Commission has turned its attention to competition in such sectors as international air transport, postal and telecommunications services, all areas in which its jurisdiction is liable to come into contact with that of competition authorities in other countries.

It was in this context that I outlined in February 1990 the principles of a co-operation agreement which I proposed should be negotiated with the USA. This suggestion was taken up by the Americans, and within barely ten months of our first contacts the Agreement was concluded on 23 September 1991. Being an administrative agreement, it does not give rise to or require any change in the laws of the parties. But within those confines, which are expressly recognised in the Agreement, it provides for co-operation in a number of areas, including notifications to the other party when actions are taken affecting its important interests, consultation and mutual assistance. To some extent these provisions resemble the principles of co-operation between competition authorities advanced by the OECD in a series of Recommendations beginning in 1967, the latest of which was issued in 1986. However, it is important to understand the different contexts of the latter and our recent agreement with the USA. The OECD's work was carried out in the context and the spirit of the disputes regarding extraterritorial jurisdiction mentioned earlier. The Recommendation was born out of imbalance, giving countries the possibility to make known their views about the exercise of extraterritorial jurisdiction by others, while at the same time leading on to implicit acceptance of such jurisdiction if they did not raise objections and providing a means to resolve the issue through consultation if they did. The spirit of the apparently-similar provisions in the Commission's agreement with the USA is quite different. The idea here is to seek ways of co-operating to make both parties' enforcement activities more effective. So an important aspect of our agreement is that is based, indeed conditional, upon balance between the parties, in particular in their enforcement activities. Taking the principles of notification, consultation and mutual assistance as a basis, we have in our agreement with the USA adapted them to our particular purposes and made the provisions more tightly drawn.

In the area of comity, we have built upon the principle that each jurisdiction should have regard to the important interests of the other in actually exercising competition jurisdiction. I would call this principle "negative comity", not in any pejorative sense, but as an expression of the idea that it calls for restraint on the part of competition authorities in some cases ("not doing" rather than "doing"). Of course, "negative" comity can only apply in cases where one has real discretion whether or not to act. The negative-comity label serves to differentiate it from another concept, which I now come to.

Our objective was to go beyond the types of procedure elaborated by the OECD, with two new principles. As these have been translated into the Agreement they have come to be known as "positive comity" and "who goes first". The idea of positive comity is that where the important interests of one party are being affected by restrictive business conduct in the territory of the other, it may call upon that other party to take enforcement action under its laws. The "who goes first" procedure is aimed at making enforcement more effective by avoiding, where possible, unnecessary duplication of effort. Where both parties could take enforcement action regarding a particular situation, it may be sensible to agree that only one of them should do so, taking into account the enforcement objectives of the other. We call it "who goes first", rather than just "who goes", because the party which has held back can jump in again at any time, if it finds that its interests would be better served by taking action itself.

One could sum up the Commission's competition agreement with the USA as pursuing two broad objectives: to avoid or resolve conflicts between the competition authorities of the parties, and to address more efficiently international business practices affecting either or both jurisdictions.

We shall have to see whether other such agreements can be concluded. As I have said, an important condition for arrangements of this kind is that there be balance, with equivalent rules and, above all, enforcement. For example, while there have been important recent moves towards more effective competition enforcement in Japan, I do not think that the time has yet come for us to enter into an agreement with that country.

The realities which have prompted our agreement with the USA have also attracted wider attention, and the question has been posed whether a multilateral approach should not be adopted in dealing with the issues which lie behind the more innovatory provisions we have made. At the same time, other developments have led to similar calls for a broader international approach to competition issues.

As the completion of the single market at last comes within our reach, after forty years of the Community's existence, the necessary contribution of competition policy to the creation of that market and the even more important role which it will have to play in the future in keeping the single market open and competitive have gained widespread recognition. At the same time as the achievement of the single market naturally causes us to look more beyond the Community's boundaries, it puts us in a stronger position to act effectively to contribute to the opening-up of world markets to trade and competition. And as we look back over the processes of those last forty years within the Community, it is more apparent than ever that the lessons learned have much relevance to the challenges now facing the international trade and investment system.

The drafters of the Treaty of Rome, with remarkable vision, realised that in order to create the Common Market, as the original Treaty called it, it was not sufficient to do away with barriers to trade and competition put up by governments. If tariffs and quotas could be replaced by price cartels and market-sharing agreements, little would have been achieved. Looking beyond governmental and private barriers, it was also realised that measures, both governmental and private, which distorted competition would also have to be brought under control. To achieve these objectives it was necessary to provide for common policies on restrictive agreements, abuse of dominant position, state aid, and the activities of public monopolies and companies enjoying special or exclusive rights. The one area which the drafters of the Treaty did not provide for, in the late 1950's, was a common system of merger control. But that was an omission for which they may be forgiven.[1]

The regulation of the international trading system, as it has developed through successive GATT Rounds, has progressively eliminated almost all quota restrictions and reduced average tariffs to low levels. Trade instruments have been introduced to combat the increased dangers of unfair trading as a result of falling barriers. These include measures against dumping, as well as countervailing duties to offset subsidies. It is perhaps understandable that there should be an urge on the part of governments to use, or abuse, these measures in order to offset government or private measures in other countries regarded as distorting international competition, but which are not directly dealt with by current international trade rules, or, worse still, to employ these instruments simply in order to try to gain perceived comparative advantages. At the same time, one has seen the development of trade measures not recognised by GATT, such as so-called Voluntary Restraint Agreements, which are unilateral trade measures. Recently, there have even been signs of an apparent willingness in some quarters to enter into arrangements which smacked of managed trade. It is said that this is not what was intended, but the Commission will continue to watch such situations closely.

Just as was the case with the Community, it is becoming acknowledged more and more widely at international level that to keep borders open it is not sufficient to remove external barriers, a process in which the GATT has been singularly successful. Domestic policies which distort trade and competition, as well policies toward private activities which create trade barriers or distort competition, will increasingly also need to be dealt with directly. The most serious trade and investment distortions resulting from the application or lack of application of domestic laws and policies must be targeted and remedied individually, in one way or another, as a matter of urgency. Broader thoughts or plans for the future should not be allowed to delay action which must be taken now if confidence in the benefits of an open trading system is not to be undermined. However, it is also apparent that in the longer term, international rules relating to domestic policies and the control of private restraints will have to be devised and implemented if substantial further progress towards an open trading system is to be achieved.

In fact, the GATT already contains rules addressing certain domestic policies such as subsidies. On the other hand, the Punta del Este mandate made

---

1. Merger control by the High Authority – now the Commission – was provided for in the earlier Coal and Steel Community. But that was a much more highly-integrative Treaty, in which regulation of the industries concerned was pooled and placed to a large degree outside the control of the Member States.

no provision for GATT rules on competition (opposing restrictive business practices, as they are called internationally). Yet the agreements which have been negotiated, and which we all hope will be adopted soon, include several provisions on that subject. It is as if realities pressing in on the trading system have already begun to overtake the political judgements of six years ago. Thus, there are provisions on the abuse of dominance by firms granted special or exclusive service rights, as well as the first "positive comity" type provisions in the Multilateral Steel Agreement and also in GATS. I have already mentioned the GATT subsidies code.

Recently I suggested that the time had come to begin thinking seriously about how one could frame the sort of rules on competition which the international trading system will require if it is to continue moving forward into the next century. Of course we are not about to transfer the rules of the Treaty of Rome, much less its supranational procedures, to the international stage. But *thinking* about solutions to these problems is very much a part of today's agenda. What I had in mind was to draw upon the traditional ways of doing things in the GATT, and see how one might apply this to competition policy by developing minimum rules and enforcement standards to be respected by governments. One would also need to bolster enforcement mechanisms for existing GATT disciplines in this area, and to design additional ones in areas new to the GATT.

Beyond that, one could consider which adaptations might be made in order to give recognition to the fact that, in essence, competition policy has to do with the rights and duties of firms and not just governments. In the case of subsidies this might include some procedural rights for companies which suffer the consequences of distortive aid to their competitors. They might, for example, be given the right to complain about state aid to the GATT. An impartial panel would review the matter and give a ruling. If a ruling declaring the aid illegal was not acted upon, countries could be authorised to impose countervailing duties. In the longer run we might develop a system of prior notification of aid to an appropriate GATT institution which would have to approve it before it was paid.

In the context of competition rules applicable to restrictive agreements, one would develop fairly straightforward rules, such as we have in the Community. A simple rule providing that restrictive practices so defined were unenforceable would mark considerable progress, by making the ordinary courts in all the signatory countries part of the enforcement mechanism. But clearly this would not help against covert activities such as price-fixing cartels. To cover such cases, a rule might be devised whereby governments would have to show that they had used their best endeavours, to be defined in a GATT rule, to prevent or punish illegal behaviour. In the case of mergers the idea might be to see how to resolve the increasing difficulties likely to arise for competition authorities and companies alike from a proliferation of merger-control laws in many countries.

I would mention that the OECD is very much involved in developing and testing ideas regarding the links between competition and trade policy, and we are actively engaged in those reflections. This is without doubt useful in developing wider understanding and appreciation of those matters and should be a forum for generating consensus between members on some of the basic issues which need to be tackled. However, the limits of this approach must be recognised and at the end of the day a forum with broad jurisdiction such as the GATT seems the best to produce results in the area of international competition policy.

The OECD's Committee on Competition Law and Policy provides a forum for mutual information and exchange of experience between the competition authorities of a growing range of countries. And in some quite specialised fields the organisation has been doing useful work in setting binding international rules, for example with regard to export credits and shipbuilding aid.

These then are some of the current thoughts and initiatives concerning the contribution which competition policy might make to open and competitive markets on the world stage. But the Community has not been inactive in developing these themes and putting them into practice at the regional level in Europe. It has been busy recently with two other external-relations projects within Europe which are of major importance and in which competition policy has a central place. It is only natural that the Community should expect from its trading partners the same strong commitment to competition policy as it itself displays, and to pursue that objective in its agreements with them where possible.

We have recently submitted to the Court of Justice a modified version of the Agreement for the creation of a European Economic Area which will bring together the Community and the EFTA countries. From the outset, it was recognised that the establishment and enforcement of identical rules of competition throughout the EEA was of central importance for the creation of an area in which the free movement of goods, services, people and capital would be fully realised. We therefore set out not only to have the same competition provisions through the "export" of the complete *acquis communautaire* to the whole of the EEA, but also to ensure the same future interpretation of the competition rules. At the same time, this had to be consistent with the fundamental political option in favour of two enforcement "pillars", and the single regulatory-control principle.

We therefore envisaged a mixed EEA Court to review EFTA "pillar" decisions, which would include judges from the Community and from the EFTA countries. The Court of Justice was called upon to give an opinion on the draft agreement. It considered that the EEA Court idea would not guarantee identical interpretation to its own. This was important because, under the single regulatory-control principle, the EFTA Surveillance Authority would be dealing with cases which at present come under the Commission's jurisdiction. Certainly, the EEA Court and the Court of Justice would be interpreting the same rules and would have several judges in common. But they would be giving their interpretations in different contexts. It cannot be denied that the context of Community competition rules has had a great deal to do with the way they have been interpreted, not least in a recent line of cases concerning Articles 86 and 90.

The solution we have now come to with our EFTA partners is to ensure that any case which would have fallen within the scope of the EC competition rules, in the absence of the EEA agreement, will be attributed to the EC "pillar". In practice this means that the Commission and the Court of Justice will fully retain the powers they have now. But in assessing the compatibility of the practice with the competition rules, the Commission and the Commission alone will have to consider the impact on competition anywhere in the EEA. In essence, the Community institutions will be responsible in the vast majority of cases for the enforcement of the competition rules throughout the nineteen countries.

Likewise, the Commission will be empowered to apply the Merger Regulation whenever a concentration is of "Community dimension" as currently defined. But in examining such a concentration, it will have to assess not only whether it creates or strengthens a dominant position and significantly impedes effective competition within the Community, but also whether it does so in any substantial part of the EEA as a whole.

The EEA agreement in fact extends the full panoply of Community competition policy to the EFTA countries, including the Community's state-aid disciplines. On the EC side, we have made a political commitment through a joint declaration appended to the EEA agreement that "financial support to undertakings financed by the EC Structural Funds or receiving assistance from the European Investment Bank or from any other similar financial instrument or fund shall be in keeping with the provisions" of the EEA Agreement. Article 90 will also extend to public companies and companies enjoying special or exclusive rights in the EFTA countries.

In view of the fact that there is no longer provision for a common EEA Court, decisions of the EFTA pillar will now be reviewed by an EFTA Court. This arrangement theoretically might not be quite as effective in future in ensuring equal conditions of competition throughout the EEA. Any divergence would be dealt with through the mechanisms for co-operation and consultation between the partners. In the particular case of state aid, a specific safeguard provision has now been included to deal with the event that one party might consider a decision of the other did not ensure equal conditions of competition throughout the EEA. The aggrieved party will be entitled to take appropriate interim measures and if a satisfactory solution is not found through consultation in the EEA Joint Committee, it will be free to take definitive measures to offset the distortion.

Perhaps the greatest benefit which will flow from the EEA agreement resides in the two-pillar approach and the close co-operation called for. Both the EEC and the EFTA countries will be able to rely on the effective *enforcement* of competition rules throughout the area, in a manner which will ensure a level playing-field in the nineteen countries as far as competition policy is concerned.

The other initiative which I wish to mention is the conclusion of "Europe Agreements" with the Czech and Slovak Federal Republic, Hungary and Poland.

The commercial provisions of these accords, under an interim arrangement, entered into force on 1 March 1992. They include provisions identical to Articles 85 and 86, as well as a prohibition similar to that in Article 92 of the Treaty concerning state aid. It is remarkable that the Agreements require in effect that these rules be applied and interpreted in accordance with the Community's practice under the corresponding Articles of the EEC Treaty. The Agreements require implementing rules for the competition and state-aid provisions to be agreed between the parties within three years. We shall be working now to establish those rules as soon as possible, preferably well before the end of that period. In the meantime, there are specific interim procedures regarding state aid of the kind I have just outlined. The proper application of the competition rules by the parties will be dealt with for the time being through the Agreements' consultative processes.

It is important to realise that the competition and aid provisions are not limited in their application to trade between the countries concerned and the Community. The rules will catch any situations which are "liable to affect" such trade. In addition, each of the countries concerned is rapidly developing its own internal competition policy. The Commission is involved in providing technical support to these countries to assist them in that process, and we are now developing ideas for co-operation on a firm and long-term footing.

Recently, the Community has begun negotiations with Romania and Bulgaria on the conclusion of similar agreements to those which we now have with Czechoslovakia, Hungary and Poland.

Conclusion

Thus, the international dimension of the Community's competition policy has developed beyond recognition in a very short space of time. It has contributed, and will continue to contribute, to the immense changes taking place in our continent and to preparing for the Europe of the 21st century. At the same time, it faces a range of vital and challenging issues for the development of international economic relations in the world at large.

8. Reducing regional disparities in the Community

A new context for old ideas

The European Community's long-standing commitment to ensuring "harmonious development by reducing the differences existing between the various regions and the backwardness of the less-favoured regions" has received a new impetus in recent years, and a new name: cohesion. The Maastricht Treaty added a special protocol reasserting that the attainment of economic and social cohesion was "vital to the full development and enduring success of the Community", and provided for a Fund to develop the Community's action in promoting cohesion. This increased emphasis on cohesion puts it at the top of the Community agenda and makes it one of our main priorities. In addition, the Treaty reiterated Article 130b of the Single European Act requiring account to be taken of cohesion in the formulation and implementation of Community policies.

Recognition of the fact that cohesion must involve all Community policies, not just the spending of the Structural Funds, therefore lies at the heart of a new approach which requires an assessment of the impact of each policy decision on the less-favoured regions and a need to tailor it to take account of cohesion. Competition policy has a special role to play in this respect, particularly as far as state aid is concerned.

State aid and the emphasis on regional development

Article 92 of the Treaty of Rome sets out the principle that state aid is incompatible with the common market "save as otherwise provided in this Treaty". The article goes on immediately to define a number of purposes for which aid is or may be justified. It is striking that in the small number of categories where the Commission *may* approve aid, the objective of fostering regional development features twice: Article 92.3(a) deals with "aid to promote the economic development of areas where the standard of living is abnormally low or where there is serious underemployment", and Article 92.3(c) provides for "aid to facilitate the development ... of certain economic areas, where such aid does not adversely affect trading conditions to an extent contrary to the common interest".

Over the years, and particularly from the 1970's onwards, the Commission has developed its ideas on the contribution its state-aid policy can make to reducing regional disparities in the Community through a large number of decisions and a series of policy statements and guidelines. Looking back over the last twenty years, I see the development of this side of competition policy as

57

falling into two periods. First, approximately from 1970 to 1985, the codification of the ruling allowing state aid for regional development took place. During this time the contribution of competition policy to the weaker regions was primarily seen as coming through control of regional aid in the richer regions. Second, from 1985 onwards, there was an increasing recognition of the regional impact of all aid spending, including schemes with horizontal and/or specific objectives which in themselves had nothing to do with regional development. In this most recent period increasing attention has been paid to the beneficial impact on the weakest regions of a reduction of aid spending generally, for regional but also for other purposes in the more prosperous regions. This recognition has brought about changes in previous policy decisions designed to bring current policy into line with the reinforced objective of cohesion.

A little history: 1970-1985

In October 1971 the Council adopted a Resolution[1] based on a Commission Communication on the co-ordination of general systems of regional aid. The terms of the Commission's Communication have an uncannily familiar ring twenty years on:

> The Member States and the Community institutions have laid stress on the need to end the competition for investment by means of regional aid to co-ordinate such aid schemes at Community level. This need has become more acute since the adoption by the Council and the representatives of the governments of the Member States of the resolution on the progressive establishment of economic and monetary union, for the realisation of such a union implies co-ordination of state aid.
>
> The last few years, and especially the period since the completion of the customs union, have seen a sharp increase in the volume and impact of state aid, and general regional aid schemes in particular. Not only are the Member States stepping up their use of such instruments in the conduct of their economic development policies, but the effects of such intervention on competition and trade are being felt more strongly as customs barriers disappear.

The purpose of the Resolution was to recognise the essential role of regional aid in regional development and to deal with the risk of outbidding between regions and Member States (outbidding refers to competition between regions using

---

1. *OJ C* 111, 4 November 1971.

offers of aid to attract mobile investment). The Resolution set out four main principles which still guide policy today: first, a single ceiling for aid intensity, which applied to all regional aid granted for a particular investment; second, transparency; third, regional specificity, which meant that regional aid could not cover the whole of the national territory, that the boundaries of the regions benefiting from aid were to be clearly defined, and that aid was to be varied according to the urgency and intensity of problems, not granted in a pinpoint manner (i.e. to isolated geographical points having practically no influence on the development of a region); and fourth, consideration of the sectoral repercussions of this type of aid.

In 1975[2] and 1979[3] the Commission issued further Communications informing Member States of the principles of co-ordination which it would apply in dealing with their regional aid schemes. By 1979 the original Community of six had become nine so there was a need to provide new rules to deal with the changes arising from enlargement.

The 1979 Principles of Co-ordination expanded the 1971 emphasis on fixed investment to include alternative measures based on ecu per job created, indicated reservations about the compatibility of operating aid and introduced a method of co-ordinating aid given for the transfer of establishments. Maximum ceilings were fixed as follows:

-       the Republic of Ireland, Northern Ireland, the Mezzogiorno (southern Italy), West Berlin and the French Overseas Departments (DOMs): 75% net grant equivalent (nge) of initial investment or 13,000 ECU per job;

-       certain parts of France, Italy, and the UK: 30% nge or 5,500 ECU per job;

-       the border with East Germany (Zonenrandgebiet) and parts of Denmark: 25% nge or 4,500 ECU per job;

-       other aided areas: 20% nge or 3,500 ECU per job.

The 1979 Co-ordination Principles set the outer limits of acceptability. The Commission spent the next few years devising a method for evaluating regional aid which would be common to all regions, easy to apply and based on harmonised EC statistics so that there was equal treatment of regions between Member States. The method, still used today, was adopted in 1983, but was not published until 1988.[4] Applying Article 92.3(c) - the derogation allowing aid to "facilitate the development of certain economic areas" - it is designed to examine the socio-economic situation of each region in its national and Community context. If a predetermined significant regional disparity is shown

2. COM(75) 77 final of 26.2.75.

3. *OJ C* 31, 3 February 1979.

4. *OJ C* 212, 12 August 1988.

to exist, aid may be granted. The main socio-economic indicators used are GDP per head and structural unemployment. The statistical criteria are regularly updated. The two indicators provide the basis for an analysis which is then completed by an examination of other relevant indicators, such as migration and demographic pressure, to bring the situation of each region into more precise focus.

On the basis of these general criteria and its method, the Commission took a number of individual decisions on national regional aid schemes. These decisions set the geographical boundaries of eligible areas, and a variety of intensity ceilings - often lower than those set out in the Co-ordination Principles, so that aid was differentiated according to the degree of structural handicap of the region. Currently some 23% of the EC's population live in regions approved for regional assistance under Article 92.3(c).

More recent history: from 1985 to today

History rolled on and the Community was again enlarged, first in 1981 to admit Greece and then in 1986 to admit Spain and Portugal. By now it was clear that the range of levels of regional development was much greater than had ever been known in the original six Member States (with the exception of the Mezzogiorno) and that once again a new situation called for a new approach. The Commission decided in 1987 to activate Article 92.3(a).[5] In their wisdom and foresight, the EC's founding fathers had put an article in the Treaty which seemed to be precisely designed to meet the needs of countries such as Greece, Portugal and Ireland. Until the 1980's Article 92.3(a) had rarely been used and no one had ever attempted to interpret its meaning in a general way.

It was decided to use a single economic indicator - GDP per head expressed in terms of purchasing-power parity - to encapsulate the problems of abnormally-low living standards and unemployment. The cut-off point was set at 75, i.e. regions coming under Article 92.3(a) have a GDP of 75% or less of the EC average. (Northern Ireland and the Spanish region of Teruel were included even though their respective GDPs exceeded 75%.) These regions currently account for around 18% of the EC population of 340 million people. It was decided to retain the 75% top intensity level from the 1979 Co-ordination Principles for 92.3(a) areas and the Commission also used the opportunity to set out its views on the range of aid instruments which could be used in these areas. In addition to the usual investment and job-creation aid, the Commission explained that it would consider approving certain forms of operating aid provided it was limited in time, was designed to promote the durable and balanced development of economic activity, and did not give rise to sectoral over-capacity at the Community level. In 1988 this method was used to define eligibility for Objective 1 of the Community's reformed Structural Funds, and the list of "political" exceptions was extended by the Council of Ministers.

---

5. *Ibid.*

Developments in the late 1980's

Two national examples serve to illustrate the recent policy of the Commission towards national regional aid.

Italy

Having adopted its new 92.3(a) method in 1987, the Commission applied it to Italy in its first-ever comprehensive review of the aid system in operation in the Mezzogiorno. The result of the analysis was that 30 of the 39 provinces were accorded 92.3(a) status, but the nine most northerly parts of the Mezzogiorno were subject to much closer scrutiny in view of their higher levels of development. In 1988 the Commission decided that aid should be phased out in two of them by the end of 1990, and in two more by the end of 1992; it should be reduced to 30% in a further province by the end of 1990 and the situation in the four provinces of the Abruzzi should be reviewed by the end of 1990 (the Commission has since decided to postpone this review to the end of 1993). The point of this appraisal was to ensure that aid was differentiated according to need and that only areas with severe handicaps, measured on a Community scale, would receive the highest levels of assistance. The stricter approach reflected both the needs of competition policy in an increasingly-integrated market and cohesion policy in terms of the concentration of aid on the areas of greatest need.

West Germany

Since the early 1980's the Commission had been expressing the view that the coverage of regional aid in West Germany was excessive - in terms of the relatively low internal disparities inside the country and in terms of its relatively prosperous situation in the Community. In 1987 45% of the West German population were living in areas eligible for regional aid (48% if West Berlin is included). The Commission decided to enter into negotiations to bring this level down to levels more in keeping with the country's situation measured against the Community average.

In 1988 a first reduction was made to 38%, accompanied by a reduction in aid intensity. In 1991 a new reduction was made to 27% of the population, thus achieving a very significant reduction in a period of four years. Again in this example the Commission was guided by the twin concerns of competition and cohesion. The process of revising downwards the level of aid coverage in the more developed parts of the Community continues to be a key element of policy.

State-aid policy and the reduction of regional disparities

At this stage it may be useful to spell out a little more clearly the practical contribution which the control of national regional aid can make to reducing regional disparities across the Community.

National regional aid to companies[6] is aimed to attract investment into particular regions and to compensate indigenous and new firms for the handicap of being based, or setting up, there. Commission policy on national regional aid seeks a balance between the distortion of competition caused by granting aid and any offsetting advantage to the Community in the form of regional development. In considering the role of national regional aid in achieving greater cohesion, it is necessary to take account of both authorised and actual amounts. Although the Commission is prepared to authorise high levels of aid intensity for the poorest parts of the Community (up to 75% investment aid in 92.3(a) areas), the level of aid actually paid per project (even with Community co-financing) is only about half the level of the ceilings authorised by the Commission. In recent years the average aid intensity was only 40% of the approved ceiling in Ireland and the assisted areas of Spain, 50% in Portugal and Greece and 75% in the Mezzogiorno.

Two further sets of figures are very telling. First, in the aided regions of the Community's geographical centre (Germany, the centre-north of Italy, the UK and France), regional aid amounted to around 90 ECU per capita over the period 1986-88, while in the aided areas of the 92.3(a) regions it came to only 16 ECU. These figures clearly show the inadequacy of national budgetary resources for development in the poorest parts of the Community. They underline the need both for increased Community funds to compensate for the inadequacy of national funding and the need to continue downward pressure on aid in central regions.

Second, even with the doubling of the EC's Structural Funds over the period 1988-93 and their concentration on Objective 1 areas, the imbalance between rich and poor Member States is still clear. National regional aid to companies, which amounted to 12bn ECU a year in the twelve Member States over the period 1986-88, is 16 times greater than Community assistance to companies from the Regional Fund.

These figures seem to show that the availability of aid is related more to national budgetary strength than to the size of structural handicap or degree of objective need when viewed in the Community context. Therefore, unless national regional aid is strictly controlled in the more prosperous central regions and limited to areas which suffer from structural handicaps which have a Community as well as a national dimension, the richer central regions will continue to pull ahead of the poorer ones. This will happen not just because of the existing combination of advantages, but also because of the artificial advantage of public subsidies.

National aid control and the Structural Funds

From small beginnings in the 1970's (the first budget of the European Regional Development Fund in 1975 represented 2.4% of the Community's budget)

---

6. Articles 92, 93 only apply to aid to companies. They do not normally apply to publicly-funded infrastructure projects.

Community spending on regional assistance has rapidly increased in volume and importance as the Community has expanded and as cohesion has become one of its priorities (accounting for 12.3% of the 1992 budget). As its own policies and spending have grown, the Commission has been called upon to consider the coherence between its competition and Structural Fund policies and to dovetail the two.

Structural Fund policy has a single goal - to develop problem regions in the Community, ideally to the point where they no longer need assistance because sufficient broadly-spread development has been achieved to allow them to face the future with their own resources. State-aid policy shares this purpose, but from a different perspective. All state aid, including regional aid, distorts competition and can only be allowed if the distortion can be shown to be outweighed by the contribution the aid makes to the common, i.e. Community, interest. Thus a balance must be found between the distortion of competition and any offsetting Community advantage and this balance may be judged from the Community as well as the national point of view. Therefore, in addition to its responsibility for fostering cohesion, competition policy carries the burden of ensuring that distortions of competition are reduced to a minimum.

Structural Fund and state-aid policies have different starting points. Since their reform, the Structural Funds have operated on the basis of providing assistance in regions which meet predetermined criteria according to a limited number of broad objectives. They are directed by the Commission, but in active partnership with the national authorities and regional and local interest-groupings at every stage. Most Regional Fund assistance is for infrastructure projects and comparatively little is paid to companies. Out of ERDF commitments of 3.7bn ECU for the period 1986-88, 2.7bn was for infrastructure.

State-aid policy is essentially reactive. Member States decide, as part of their internal economic and social policies, on the aid they wish to grant, and the role of the Commission is to decide whether such aid may be allowed in the interest of the Community. It has always been considered as a legitimate part of the common interest to allow each Member State to have a national policy for regional development, on the basis that reducing internal national disparities contributes to more balanced economic development. If, as I believe it should, this basic principle is to continue to guide Commission policy, it is necessary to evaluate national regional aid from a national as well as a Community point of view. Even in the most prosperous Member States there can be problem regions which are significantly below the national average when measured in terms of a variety of socio-economic indicators, e.g. employment and level of income. National assistance to these regions may be justified even where the problems are not sufficiently serious to warrant an intervention by the Community's limited funds. Such an approach, which is based on the principle of subsidiarity, will inevitably produce some areas which are eligible for national regional aid, but not eligible for Structural Fund assistance (currently around 10% of the EC's population).

Structural Fund assistance needs to be concentrated in order to produce maximum effect. The question has been raised, however, as to whether it is coherent to have a situation where the Structural Funds intervene in areas which are not (or are no longer) eligible for national regional aid (5% of the EC's population). This question is a fairly recent one. For example, before the reform of the Structural Funds, eligibility for national regional aid was a precondition of eligibility for Regional Fund assistance[7] and similar conditions pertained in principle to the ERDF non-quota steel, shipbuilding, and textile programmes and to RESIDER. The question of geographical coherence, therefore, did not really arise. The current regulations only require conformity of Structural Fund action with other Community policies, including competition, and thus leave open the possibility for the Structural Funds to intervene outside nationally-assisted areas.

These situations arise mainly in Objective 2 (industrial decline) and 5(b) (rural development) regions. In order to ensure coherence between its policies, the Commission has decided to divide the regions of the Community into four: i) regions where no regional aid is allowed (53% of the EC's population); ii) regions where only national aid is allowed (+/- 10%); iii) regions where national aid is, in principle, not allowed but which are eligible for Structural Fund assistance (5%; in these regions, as an exception to the normal competition rules, Member States may request authorisation to give aid to small and medium-sized companies, and to promote tourism, handicrafts, etc.); and iv) regions eligible for both national and EC aid (38%).

The Commission has recently launched its general ideas for Structural Fund spending for the period 1993-97. It is now beginning to work out key questions such as eligibility criteria for the period after 1993. It has reaffirmed its commitment to maintaining concentration as defined in geographical and spending terms. In my opinion, in view of the population and spending figures which I have quoted, it is desirable to reinforce concentration, not just maintain it. I will continue to argue in the Commission for greater geographical concentration of Structural Fund spending because I believe concentrating on the weakest regions is essential from the point of view of cohesion and that too great a spread of aid reduces its impact and efficiency.

There will be a need to review again our policy on national regional aid, both to make sure that it continues to be an effective part of competition policy and to make it as coherent as possible with the development of the Structural Funds. There can be no question of one policy playing a subordinate role to the other: each will have to be adjusted to take appropriate account of the operation of the other.

The regional impact of non-regional aid

It is clear that state aid must be analysed not just in relation to its professed or primary purpose, but also in the wider context of its impact on competition and

---

7. Regulation EEC 1787/84 of 19 June 1984, Articles 11.3 and 17.

regional development. All aid is paid to companies located in specific geographical areas, so it can be said that all aid has a regional impact. In dealing with general or horizontal schemes it is useful for the Commission to know their regional impact. However, even today we know relatively little about the cross-effects of aid. For example, most national R & D aid is concentrated on companies in the most prosperous regions of the Community. Does this have an anti-regional impact? We do not know enough about cross-effects, but are putting in place the means of finding out their real impact.

Greater information on cross-effects is vital if the Commission is to ensure that they do not inadvertently negate the impact of other policies. Later this year I will be proposing to the Commission the introduction of standardised annual reporting on all aid schemes in operation in the Member States. The reports will cover three budgetary years and will have to include a regional and sectoral breakdown of spending as well as the names and number of beneficiaries. Once this information becomes available it will be possible for the Commission to deal better with cross-effects and to take account of them in future aid decisions.

Where it is already evident that schemes give rise to harmful cross-effects, action is being taken. The First and Second Aid Surveys published in 1989 and 1990 provided the first comprehensive accounts of spending on aid and an opportunity to compare aid levels and patterns between Member States. The information available in the Surveys clearly pointed to a need to review existing aid schemes, in particular those used to promote general investment. The Commission decided that such schemes, which had no clear regional or other objective, posed the greatest threat to intra-Community trade and competition. Such aid had become either a general investment stimulus when applied widely or, when applied more selectively, simply a means of intervening on an ad hoc basis. In July 1990 the Commission adopted a decision of principle, to the effect that general investment aid in one Member State could eliminate the incentive effect of regional aid offered in another, as well as in the assisted areas of the same Member State; such aid adversely affected competition and cohesion and should be abolished. In a series of individual decisions the Commission asked the Netherlands, Belgium and Luxembourg to abolish their general schemes. As a result of this policy, the Dutch Government has abolished a scheme with an annual budget of 26m ECU and Belgium a similar scheme which was costing 96m ECU in 1990. The Luxembourg authorities have also accepted the recommendation to abolish their scheme and other Member States are revising their schemes to bring them into line with current policy.

Other competition-policy contributions to cohesion

I have concentrated so far on the role of state-aid policy in promoting cohesion in the Community. However, other aspects of competition policy have a crucial contribution to make to combatting the costs associated with peripherality and lower levels of development. One example will suffice here.

Many of the Community's poorest regions suffer from higher transport and communications costs, which hamper their development. At the same time, there is a great pent-up demand waiting to be released in the telecommunications market. More competition would mean cheaper prices, better service and a greater range of services. The Commission has already used its powers to open up the market for telecommunications equipment and certain services, but has left the monopoly on voice telephony untouched. In my opinion, the time has come to reconsider the justification for such monopolies which, it can be argued, limit the market and impose high costs on industrial users. The European Consumers' Organisation, BEUC, has just published a study of price differences and variations in quality of service in Europe's telephone system. On average, Spain and Ireland have the most expensive international calls in the EC. The cost of telecommunications can be an important factor for businesses in disadvantaged areas, particularly where many firms are involved in export markets. Reduced telecommunications charges reduce the costs of locating in the periphery - in fact cheap and efficient telecommunication systems reduce peripherality itself, not physically, but in terms of its consequences. Therefore, while all of European industry would benefit from liberalisation, I believe the weakest regions on the periphery would benefit disproportionately. A similar case can be made for liberalisation of the air-transport and energy sectors - both areas where the Commission is pushing ahead.

Future policy development

Progress towards economic and social cohesion and the narrowing of the gap between Europe's regions has become a central objective, and one which will stay at the top of the Community's agenda. Competition policy will continue to need adjusting to realise the full contribution it can make to achieving this major goal. I will outline three new policy initiatives which I am planning to bring forward this year and to explain how they will contribute to reducing regional disparities.

a) *A framework for aid to small and medium-sized companies.* The Commission has a generally positive attitude towards aid for SMEs. In the interests of transparency and in order to bring about greater coherence between schemes in different Member States, I will be proposing an aid framework to the Commission, setting out the circumstances in which, and the extent to which, such aid will be permitted. One of the issues posed is the extent to which we should also allow investment aid for SMEs outside already-assisted areas. Given the Commission's negative attitude towards general investment aid, I believe allowing such aid to medium-sized companies in non-assisted areas also runs counter to the policy of cohesion by reducing the attractiveness of the incentives offered in assisted areas. I will therefore be proposing to limit investment aid outside assisted areas to small companies, defined as those having fewer than 50 employees and a turnover of less than 5m ECU.

b) *Cumulation of aid*. In 1985 the Commission set out rules[8] governing the cumulation of aid for different purposes, e.g. to deal with situations where an SME investing in an assisted region and carrying out R & D might benefit under three different aid schemes (regional, SME and R & D aid). Once again, the greater availability of budgetary resources in the more prosperous Member States means that the possibility of "topping up" regional aid is greater in central regions. For example, between 1986-88, in the UK, Benelux, France, Italy and Germany, aid for SMEs represented 16% of spending on aid to the manufacturing sector and general investment aid a further 7%, giving 23% in total. This compares with 4-5% for the same purposes in the 92.3(a) areas. These figures illustrate the reasons which led the Commission to propose the abolition of general investment aid in central regions and the need for a framework for SME aid. I am far from satisfied that the current rules are working to deliver their original purpose of controlling the application of more than one aid scheme to a given investment project so as to ensure that intensity levels do not rise above acceptable limits. Therefore I am considering changes to the present system which will ensure that cumulation limits work effectively.

c) *Capital-intensive aid*. The fact that high levels of regional aid are authorised for the poorest regions (even if, as we have seen, they are not always paid, owing to budgetary constraints) can give rise to competition problems, particularly in dealing with capital-intensive investment. The Commission has decided to tackle this problem and I am currently considering the introduction of new rules which will significantly reduce the competition-distorting effects of such aid without impairing the ability of the poorest regions to attract such investment. One idea currently under consideration would be to introduce a ceiling on eligible investment per job created and then to use the existing regional aid ceilings to calculate the maximum aid which could be granted. In practical terms such a system, for example based on a ceiling of 175,000 ECU of eligible investment per job, would mean for the same investment of 1bn ECU creating 50,000 jobs that a region with a ceiling of 45% could offer 394m ECU for the project and a 20% region could offer 175m ECU. Under the current system the 45% region would have had to offer 450m ECU and the 20% region 200m ECU if both felt they had to offer the maximum aid to win the project. Thus a modified system would reduce spending, leaving more money in the national budget for other purposes (an important consideration for the poorer Member States) while maintaining the incentive effect of the aid which works in favour of the poorer regions. Proposals on this issue will be discussed with Member States and I hope the Commission will adopt new rules before the end of 1992.

Conclusion

The aim of this survey of the interconnections between competition policy and

8. *OJ C* 3, 5 January 1985.

cohesion has been to show how closely related they are and how a strict state-aid policy can contribute in important ways to reducing regional disparities. This aspect of the policy has become more marked in recent years as the central importance of cohesion has been recognised. Nonetheless, much work remains to be done before the original aspiration of the Treaty of Rome to aim for "the constant improvement of the living and working conditions of their peoples" and to reduce "the differences existing between the various regions and the backwardness of the less-favoured regions" can become a reality.

9. Post and telecommunications

Efficient postal and telecommunications services are essential to the success of the single-market programme and the providers of these services are in turn direct beneficiaries of market expansion. We are all users of postal and telecommunications services on a daily basis. They account for 3% of Community GDP and employ more than 2.5 million people. It is evident that the economic significance of open markets in this area is considerable.

Before turning specifically to the postal and telecommunications sectors, I should like to paint in the background to the Community's competition policy as it relates to those areas where firms enjoy special or exclusive rights within their sector.

Competition policy in the area of monopolies

It is quite clear from the terms of the Treaty of Rome that the continued existence of monopolies was seen as the exception rather than the rule. National monopolies are contrary to the basic concept of a common market which implies the free circulation of goods and services between the Member States. The provisions of the Treaty which do allow for their continued existence are attempts, to one degree or another, to limit the extent of their application.

Of particular interest in the context of this chapter is Article 90 of the Treaty, which some have likened to a bludgeon, but which I prefer to see as a scalpel in the hand of a skilled surgeon. It is an important provision of the Treaty and is both permissive and limitative. It clearly establishes that there are limits to the extent and nature of the rights which can be reserved. Member States may not enact laws or keep existing laws on the statute books if they are in any way contrary to the Treaty rules. Moreover, it goes on to declare unequivocally that the Treaty's competition rules apply to all firms entrusted with a service of general economic interest.

At the same time, it permits an exception where the application of the Treaty rules would obstruct the performance of the task assigned to such a firm. The net effect of this exception is to relate and limit the special or exclusive rights reserved to a firm to those, and only those, necessary to achieve its task of general economic interest. Even then, the interests of the Community in the development of trade take precedence over the rights of the firm.

Lastly, and of great significance, Article 90 (3) imposes a duty on the Commission to police the application of this provision. The Commission has no discretion in the matter.

That is not to say that the Commission is a reluctant policeman. The proper functioning of the internal market, which is of benefit to the whole

Community, can only be achieved through the correct and timely implementation of the Treaty provisions and the Commission cannot, therefore, be less than vigilant in its actions. And Article 90 (3) provides us with the means to act - the Commission "shall, where necessary, address appropriate directives or decisions to the Member States".

This the Commission has done in a number of cases. In the telecommunications sector, for example, it has issued directives under Article 90 (3) relating to competition in the markets for terminal equipment and for services, which I will examine later. Moreover, the Court of Justice has supported the Commission's decision to employ Article 90 (3) as a basis for taking such action in a case taken by the French Government relating to the terminal-equipment directive. It also confirmed that the Commission has far-reaching powers to prevent governments restricting competition by conferring monopoly or other special rights when this is not justified on genuine public-service grounds. Armed now with judicial approval, it is inevitable that the Commission will increasingly consider the option of using Article 90 as a basis for examining the activities of those sectors currently under review and of others as yet untouched.

While it is essential that those sectors in which companies enjoy special or exclusive rights be subject to the rules on competition if the internal market is to function properly, the Commission also recognises the importance of basic services such as electricity, water, post and telecommunications being supplied universally. The Commission has stressed on several occasions that they should remain accessible and affordable to all, with good quality of service and security of supply.

The task therefore facing the Commission is to open up competition in these areas while ensuring that the activities of general economic interest can be performed. In responding to this problem, the Community has adopted the approach of liberalisation coupled with the harmonisation of standards and quality in order to increase consumer choice and value for money. By looking at the postal and telecommunications sectors, we can see how this has been addressed in practice.

Telecommunications

Commentators on Community telecommunications policy frequently confuse two areas: Community telecommunications policy and Community competition policy as applied to the telecommunications industry. The first is based on the power of the Commission to propose to the Council of Ministers any measure which it deems necessary to achieve a common market. This may be started by means of consultative documents - Green Papers - or policy papers - White Papers. On the basis of the comments received, the Commission then proposes draft legislation to the Council of Ministers, through a complex procedure which also involves the European Parliament. A Green Paper was adopted by the Commission in 1987 on telecommunications and forms the basis for many of the initiatives taken, and still to be taken, in this sector.[1]

Community competition policy, on the other hand, is based on specific provisions of the EEC Treaty (Articles 85, 86 and 90), entrusting the Commission, in its own right, with the power to tackle restrictive agreements and abuses of dominant position or measures by Member States imposing behaviour tantamount to such practices.

The main consequence of the distinction between these two policies is that the Commission will usually follow a twofold approach. It will itself implement existing competition rules, but will work with the Council of Ministers - representing the Member States - to establish a new legal framework for the telecommunications industry in the Community. This approach can best be illustrated by a brief review of the achievements of both policies in the past five years in the areas of equipment and services.

Terminal equipment
The first focus of the Community was the terminal market. Article 30 of the EEC Treaty prevents Member States from hindering the free circulation of goods. The maintenance of the exclusive right of national telecommunications organisations to supply terminal equipment to their "captive" customers was clearly contrary to this provision. Furthermore, it tied the service to the terminal and a customer could not have one without the other. This was also contrary to the Treaty competition rules. For this reason, in 1988 the Commission issued a Directive under its own powers (Article 90) to abolish these exclusive rights.[2] To date, the directive has been implemented by all Member States, except one, which is in the course of doing so.

While this Directive allows for the free circulation of terminal equipment, it still does not grant the right to connect such equipment to all telecommunications networks in the Community. These networks are in fact technically different. As a consequence, terminal equipment which is type-approved in one Member State still needs type-approval in each other Member State to circulate in the Community.

To tackle this problem, the Council of Ministers issued a directive on the mutual recognition of type-approvals in 1991. The Directive provides that terminal equipment which has been type-approved under European Standards in one Member State and carries an EC mark may be marketed throughout the Community without further formalities. The effective implementation of this Directive also depends on the availability of European standards and indirectly on the technical harmonisation of the networks in the Community.

Services
Let us turn now to telecommunications services, starting with the landmark Commission decision of 1982 against British Telecom. BT had refused to allow

---

1. Communication by the Commission, *Towards a Dynamic European Economy: Green Paper on the Development of the Common Market for Telecommunications Services and Equipment,* COM(87) 290 final, 30 June 1987.

2. Directive 88/301/EEC, *OJ L* 131, 27 May 1988.

telex messages originating from the European continent to be redirected through private operators in the UK to the USA. The Commission considered that such a refusal by a firm in a dominant market position, which limited technological progress, violated EC competition rules.

Taking a wider view, the Commission issued a directive in 1990 abolishing the special and exclusive right to provide telecommunications services granted by the Member States to their telecommunications organisations. At the heart of this Directive was the principle that network providers in a dominant position may not restrict the use of their networks as regards the provision of services by third parties. However, given the importance of the public voice-telephony service for the revenues of the Community telecommunications organisations, the Commission allowed the maintenance of exclusive rights for this service in order not to jeopardise the universal service. A review is under way to see if this is still justified.

The abolition of special and exclusive rights is not in itself sufficient to guarantee genuine competition in the Community because it does not prevent telecommunications organisations, acting by themselves, from restricting competition and does not automatically open up distinct national markets. We therefore issued "Competition Guidelines" in September 1991, building on the experience gained in the implementation of the competition rules in individual cases, to clarify the obligation of market participants stemming from Community competition rules. Telecom companies now have a clearer idea of what is and is not allowed in the way of agreements, co-operation arrangements and pricing. In addition, the Council has launched the Open Network Provision programme to lay down harmonised standards and conditions of access to national networks and has extended to network equipment the rules already in operation for public procurement in other sectors.

Future Community policy

The review we are now carrying out looks at the remaining monopoly rights. It will involve lengthy consultation and the Commission will not take any final decision on the outcome of the review until it is completed. The Commission's assessment will be based on the following two considerations.

Despite what has already been achieved, bottlenecks for trans-European services and networks remain. For example, intra-Community tariffs are still excessive. A 4-minute call over 100km in France costs 1.25 ECU. The same call, for the same distance but crossing a French border, costs 2.17 ECU - nearly double. Similar figures could be given for the other Member States. The high cost of crossing frontiers is only partially due to the cost of the use of international telephone exchanges.

On the other hand, it is vital to guarantee a universal service. When monopoly rights are abolished there is a risk that both the former monopoly and the new competitors will concentrate on the most profitable business users, neglecting residential subscribers. The implementation of a harmonised set of trans-European services is a justifiable public-service requirement. It could, however, be provided in a number of different ways, not necessarily by state-owned monopolies.

In my view, then, the review should focus on voice-telephony services and networks. As I have said, public voice-telephony was excluded from the 1990 directive's market liberalisation because of its importance for revenue generation and the maintenance of universal service. The Commission should now reassess this position, given the growing need for more efficient intra-Community corporate communications and the vastly-increased requirement for continent-wide networks in the new European environment. The liberalisation of public voice-telephony services between the Member States and of supporting networks as far as necessary to allow for genuine competition may contribute to meeting these needs and requirements.

I do not wish to prejudge the outcome of the review. However, I can say with confidence that the current one will not be the last. In a dynamic and innovatory sector such as this, the Commission must be prepared to stand back periodically and look objectively at progress made and areas remaining to be explored. In other words, the process launched by the Commission is only at an initial stage and telecommunications users will continue to demand lower prices, wider choice and better services. These will only be supplied to the extent that the regulatory framework allows for competing firms to design new services, to try out new technology and to assess how to provide existing services at a lower cost than the incumbent operator.

Postal services

Much of what I have said as regards competition policy in the telecommunications sector is equally applicable to the postal service, and the experience already gained there will undoubtedly influence our manner of proceeding. Here again, the Commission has adopted a twofold approach, on the one hand applying existing competition rules and on the other working with the Member States, through the Council of Ministers, to develop an appropriate regulatory framework - the first step being the preparation of the Green Paper on postal services, at the request of the Council.[3]

The emergence of competition has occurred very late in this sector and it remains one of the least liberalised in the Community today. However, the growth of private operators in recent years, especially in the express mail sector, has put the spotlight firmly on national postal authorities and their ability to provide the services their customers require. The Commission has been called upon to examine a series of cases relating to international express mail where postal authorities hindered the performance of services which they themselves were unable to provide to the same degree.

The first substantial complaint concerned the German Bundespost. The Commission found that the Bundespost was trying to apply its monopoly rights

---

3. *Green Paper on the Development of the Single Market for Postal Services*, COM(91) 476 final, 11 June 1992.

over the transport of mail to a whole range of its own services, including its own express service, Datapost. An informal intervention in 1985 led to assurances by the Bundespost that it would accept competition from international couriers in Germany and would not use below-cost tariffs to secure a position in the market.

The same year, a similar result was achieved with the French Post Office, where couriers had been taxed and limited to the Paris area. The Italian Post Office was found to favour its own express service by requiring couriers to stamp their packages and submit to checks, but it followed suit in 1989.

These particular cases represent action against Post Offices or PTTs to make them change their behaviour. They were followed by action against two governments, those of the Netherlands in 1989 and Spain in 1990. In the face of resistance, more formal procedures were adopted, leading to cease-and-desist orders. In the case of the Netherlands, a new law had fixed minimum tariffs for private couriers and required them to register their prices. The Dutch government successfully challenged the Commission decision on procedural grounds, but the judgement of the Court reinforced its earlier expressed view that Article 90 is an appropriate basis for the Commission action in this area. In Spain, international express courier services were reserved for the national Post Office even though it did not offer the full service which customers could have obtained from other operators. The Commission has also intervened with Denmark, which has agreed to change its postal law relating to international express.

In the area of cross-border letters, the focus is currently on competition for bulk business mail. Shipments of reports, statements, advertisements and so on are collected in one country, taken to another, placed in the local mail system and ultimately distributed in that country, the country of origin or a third country, a practice known as remailing. It combines private and public mail services to achieve the most efficient handling, resulting in choice and value for users and contributing to the growth of cross-border mail.

The complex issues raised by remailing have been examined in detail by the Commission in the context of a complaint from the International Express Carriers Conference against a number of Community postal authorities. The complaint is grounded on two issues. Firstly, the postal administrations concerned had agreed to raise terminal dues (the amount paid by one postal administration to another if it sends more international mail than it receives) in a way designed to deter remailing. Secondly, some of these Post Offices were said to have enforced provisions of the Universal Postal Union convention allowing them to obstruct remailing. I cannot go into the details of this case, as we have not yet reached a conclusion, but as matters stand the complaints seem to me to merit support and justify the necessary subsequent action.

The Green Paper which the Commission recently adopted is intended to clear the way for further Community action in the postal sector. At the end of the public debate, the Commission will be in a position to draw up the appropriate proposals for action. And it is certainly my intention to have achieved positive results in this regard before the end of 1992.

The Green Paper anticipates that a set of universal services, guaranteeing good quality postal service to all consumers at affordable prices, should be defined at Community level. It would allow Member States to confer a set of exclusive rights on national postal administrations in respect of certain services which they alone would perform. These would cover ordinary domestic personal and business correspondence, but with clearly-defined limits in terms of weight and price. The scope of these reserved services would have to be strictly proportional to the need to maintain the infrastructure, which for the time being is a precondition of the universal service. Where Member States can demonstrate that the permitted reserved services are insufficient to meet this need, extensions of the scope of the services granted under exclusive right may be justifiable. The competition rules to deal with any such case are already in existence and ready to test the economic arguments put forward. But I should warn here and now that it will be formidably difficult to argue for special treatment. In the interest of all postal users, it is not my intention to allow over-large monopolies to compensate for lack of competitiveness.

As I have said on previous occasions, I believe that the absolute minimum of domestic services should be reserved for monopoly providers. The aim of the Commission's proposals is to put a ring-fence around those areas reserved for postal authorities. All other areas will lie outside and will be open to free competition. These would include express mail and parcel-delivery services, which are already de facto liberalised in most Member States.

However, I would like to focus on the particular market-opening measures which have excited the greatest response in the postal world - those concerning cross-border and direct mail. The arguments for liberalising the former are considerable. It is an area where postal administrations currently give poor value as compared to their domestic services. The quality of performance often fails to reach the not-very-demanding targets for delivery, where they exist. The service is overpriced in order to compensate for the delivery costs of incoming mail. Business, which accounts for 80% of total mail, is by far the largest user of cross-border services, often by way of bulk mailing, but it is currently denied the choice and quality of service for which it is willing to pay. In addition, to maintain exclusive rights in this area would, in effect, amount to an extension of national monopolies across borders, which is unacceptable in the context of the creation of a single market.

The liberalisation of the direct-mail sector is also envisaged. This is not the radical proposal which some would claim. Competition in this area is already tolerated in many Member States. Direct mail is in fact advertising messages sent in bulk, not the unique personal messages traditionally deserving of the special protection provided by the postal administrations. It is a rapidly-expanding sector, fuelled by businesses seeking choice, value for money and good quality end-to-end service, which are not currently provided by the majority of Community postal administrations. Users are, typically, in the publishing, insurance, financial-service and mail-order sectors, although it is a valuable means for smaller companies to break into new markets, target customers and compete against established brands, without having to establish branches. The failure to ensure the choice of good-quality service would have negative consequences for those businesses relying on direct mail as a marketing technique, would discriminate against businesses established in regions where the postal service is poor and would ultimately deny their customers the same choice as their fellow Europeans. The arguments for liberalisation speak for themselves and are very persuasive.

Certain postal authorities would maintain that to liberalise these sectors would substantially undermine their ability to provide a universal service. However, one cannot assume that the Post Offices will fail to retain a considerable share of the market. After all, they are already operating in the market, with established networks and a wealth of experience to offer potential customers. The projected growth in these sectors, especially for direct mail, offers considerable promise for any postal operator able to respond to its customers' needs.

In order both to reinforce the universal service and to ensure that the services provided respond to rapidly-evolving customer needs, the Green Paper proposes a series of harmonisation measures, which are essential if we want to avoid a "two-speed" Europe.

Common rules of access should be applied in all Member States to ensure that any postal operator, be it a postal administration or private operator, wishing to exercise its right to use the network to provide services will not be obstructed by unnecessary regulatory or technical barriers.

A common tariff structure should be established, with prices for each service related to the average cost of providing that service. Moreover, the terminal dues system - the system of compensation between postal authorities in different countries - should be restructured in order to reflect the real cost of collection and delivery in the different countries.

Of particular importance for postal users, standards for performance must be set and monitored and the results published. Poor performance in the postal sector can have serious consequences for the Community's infrastructure as a whole and undermine the ability of entire regions to take full advantage of the benefits of the internal market. Moreover, the consumer has a right to value for money and to know what he or she is buying. This is all the more important for those reserved services where competition is not allowed. Postal administrations cannot enjoy exclusive rights without assuming commensurate obligations to perform the services to the highest possible quality.

Conclusion

The new proposals in the telecommunications sector, particularly those relating to voice-telephony and the postal service, provide a starting-point for further liberalisation. We need a short sharp debate on the substance, followed quickly by positive action. Measures will be implemented gradually to allow Member States the necessary time to make the appropriate adjustments. The policy approach which we have chosen for the postal and telecommunications sectors is a careful balance between liberalisation and harmonisation. In hardly any other policy area do we see such a vivid coalescence of Citizens' Europe and the Single Market.

10. The public sector

This chapter covers three separate issues: the extent to which the Treaty recognises and permits the grant of monopoly rights to a company; whether or to what extent publicly-owned companies are exempt from the application of Articles 85 and 86; and the Community's state-aid policy with respect to public companies.

The Treaty's scope for granting monopoly rights

The first of these is probably the most controversial aspect of Community competition law, because it raises issues at the cutting edge of the debate within the Community regarding sovereignty, subsidiarity and the role of the Commission as the guarantor of a truly open and competitive common market. The fact that the grant of monopoly rights normally leads to higher prices and less innovation than would result from the free operation of the market mechanism is neither new nor contested. Equally, however, there are some non-economic objectives that may rarely but legitimately lead a Member State to grant monopoly rights to a single company, usually publicly-owned. For example, the standard delivery of personal letters is reserved for the publicly-owned and operated Post Offices in all Member States. The aim is to ensure that all people, even those in remote areas, receive the same service. This social function is viewed as of even greater public interest than the maintenance of completely free competition.

One could imagine the Community playing no role in determining which services a Member State should reserve for public monopolies for non-economic reasons. However, when a Member State chooses to achieve that non-economic aim through the grant of monopoly rights the Community must play a role, for that grant inevitably limits the achievement of a true common market. For example, prior to its accession to the Community, the Spanish government had granted the exclusive right to import and sell tobacco to Tabacalera; similar rights regarding petroleum products had been granted to CEPSA. These exclusive rights had three important consequences for the common market: they limited trade between Member States, they restricted the right of establishment and they excluded competition from other Community firms. Pursuant to Article 37 of the Treaty, these exclusive rights were phased out.

It is equally true that the grant of monopoly rights for production and marketing can infringe Articles 30 and 52 of the Treaty and it is therefore not surprising that the Court has confirmed the Commission's power, through a combination of Articles 90 and 30, 52 and 86, to declare the grant of monopoly rights by a Member State incompatible with the Treaty. From the mid-1980's on, the Commission adopted several decisions and directives against exclusive rights which it considered contrary to the Treaty.

Following a complaint from professional insurers' organisations, the Commission adopted a decision in 1986 addressed to the Greek government, which had by law reserved the insurance of all public property for the Greek public companies in this sector, thereby excluding the insurance companies of all other Member States. According to the Commission this exclusive right was contrary to the prohibition in Article 52 of discrimination on grounds of nationality as regards the freedom of establishment.

A second decision, tackling exclusive rights in the Netherlands, was taken in 1989. The Dutch Postal Act prevented express courier companies providing their services in or from the Netherlands. This decision was successfully challenged on procedural grounds, but the judgment of the Court reaffirmed the view that Article 90 was an appropriate basis for Commission action in this area. A similar decision was addressed to the Spanish government regarding its definition of the postal monopoly covering all letters and documents up to 2 kg in weight, which impeded international courier companies from operating to and from Spain.

The Commission likewise took action against Germany, Italy and Belgium in respect of the exclusive rights which had been granted by their governments to their state telecommunications administrations to sell or rent certain terminal equipment such as modems, telex terminals and cordless telephones. As a result of this action, the Commission decided to act more comprehensively by adopting directives addressed to all Member States.

However, it is clear that not every grant of exclusive rights constitutes an infringement of the Treaty. Such actions may be a reasonable and necessary manner in which to provide services of general economic interest. Article 90(2) therefore provides that in such circumstances the monopoly rights may be compatible with the Treaty. They may be necessary, for example, to guarantee essential interests such as the protection of public health, the environment, or public safety.

The task facing the Commission is, therefore, one of finding the right equilibrium between the need to guarantee an open and competitive market and the need to acknowledge the right of each Member State to achieve certain non-economic objectives in the manner it sees fit. I view Article 90 as providing the Commission with a tool ideally suited to this task. It acknowledges the legitimacy of the grant of exclusive rights where this is the only reasonable economic, technical or legal manner in which to achieve the legitimate objectives in question. Thus, the Commission does not inquire into whether a non-economic objective of a Member State is in itself legitimate, but examines whether the *manner* in which that objective is pursued is proportionate to what is required, given the negative consequences that it may have on the achievement of the Community's fundamental aims. For example, the Commission reached the conclusion that the grant by certain Member States to their national post and telecommunications administrations of the exclusive right to sell telecommunications terminal equipment was contrary to Article 90 in combination with Articles 86 and 59, on the grounds that the monopoly was neither necessary nor proportionate to the aim of guaranteeing a secure and universal telephone service.

It is true that the Commission must tread carefully when examining these issues, to ensure that the correct balance is maintained between its role as guarantor of the common market and that of the Member States as guarantors of certain non-economic benefits to their citizens. It is for this reason that the Commission's action in opening up new sectors to competition is both gradual and meticulous in its preparation. One cannot predict where this process will lead us, but I believe that we have still much work to do. Let me make one observation in conclusion on this point. The question of which non-economic objectives must be pursued by a Member State and the best manner in which to achieve them is one that changes over time. I believe a recognition is spreading throughout the Community that the granting of monopoly rights to public companies is one of the least attractive ways of achieving these aims. I predict, therefore, a gradual and continual opening-up to competition of previously-reserved Community markets. We have already taken some tentative steps down this road; but there is a long way yet to go.

Exemptions for public companies from Articles 85 and 86

The starting-point for any consideration of the second issue that I wish to discuss here is a very simple statement: no company, just as no individual, is above the law. Article 90(2) recognises this, stating clearly that all publicly-owned companies, whether or not they are granted monopoly rights, are subject to the rules on competition. There is, however, a caveat: they are only subject to these Treaty Articles "in so far as the application of such rules does not obstruct the performance, in law or fact, of the particular tasks assigned to them".

Until the early 1980's public companies in the Community acted largely in disregard of Articles 85 and 86, relying on a generous interpretation of the caveat in Article 90(2). Now, however, a string of decisions has placed the respect of Community competition law on the agenda of public companies in exactly the same way as it has been the concern of private ones.

The first decision under Article 86 involving a public company was adopted in 1982. The Member State appealed against this decision on the grounds that it violated Article 222 by tackling only public companies. The Court of Justice, however, rejected this argument.

In 1985, the Court considered this issue in the context of a question posed to it pursuant to Article 177 by a Luxembourg court. RTL had been granted certain exclusive broadcasting rights by the government. Not surprisingly, the Court observed that a company, be it public or private, that is granted a legal monopoly to perform a given service, will have a dominant position within the meaning of Article 86. RTL had refused to sell advertising spots for "*télémarketing*" unless the purchaser used RTL's sales facilities. The Court stated that the use of RTL's legally-granted dominant position in one sector (broadcasting) to move into another constituted an abuse under Article 86.

In 1989, in another landmark case, the Commission applied Article 85 to the activities of the 26 members of the European Conference of Postal and Telecommunications Administrations, which had increased its recommended prices for leased international lines. Following the Commission's intervention, the Telecommunications Administrations agreed to abandon this price-fixing arrangement.

In each of these cases, the company in question attempted to invoke Article 90(2) in defence of its anti-competitive conduct. However, like any Treaty provision establishing a derogation to a basic Community norm, this Article is interpreted very strictly. In short, Article 90(2) can only excuse an infringement of Article 85 or 86 where the anti-competitive action is the only manner in which the legitimate public-service function imposed on the company in question can reasonably be achieved. There must be no other reasonable economic, technical or legal method for the company to carry out its specific task. This test, reminiscent of the Court's approach to derogations from the basic principle of Article 30 in the Cassis de Dijon judgment, is the same whether one is considering if the grant of an exclusive right in itself is compatible with the Treaty, or whether a public company's behaviour which is incompatible with Article 85 or 86 can be excused by virtue of Article 90(2).

In the latter respect, however, Article 90(2) is a very difficult test to meet, and in fact no decision exists in which a public company's action or agreement that infringed Article 85 or 86 was justified by this provision. The decision in the Ijsselcentrale case is a good example of this. An agreement between a number of Dutch electricity-generating and -distribution companies had the effect of monopolising the import and export of electricity. This agreement, which prevented trade, infringed Article 85(1). The companies attempted to invoke Article 90(2) as a defence. While the Commission accepted that the companies were legally entrusted with a service of general economic interest - the reliable and efficient operation of the national electricity supply in a socially-responsible manner - it concluded that they could perfectly well achieve these objectives without monopolising imports and exports.

In conclusion, I believe that the need to respect Articles 85 and 86 must now be fully taken into account by all publicly-owned and -operated companies, and there is no real need to differentiate between public and private in this respect. In fact, because of the approach of the Commission and the Court to Article 90(2), limiting its scope to the absolute minimum, the real effect of this Article is to justify in certain limited cases the actual grant of monopoly rights and the consequent restrictions of competition that flow directly and inevitably from that grant - the limiting of production and supply to the detriment of consumers, for example. It is more difficult to envisage cases where it could be used to justify further actions that infringe Articles 85 and 86 but which do not flow directly and inevitably from the grant of the exclusive rights. In the latter circumstances, it is difficult to believe that it is beyond human ingenuity for the company in question to achieve the same legitimate aim, but through less restrictive means.

Public companies and the state-aid rules

A system of free and undistorted competition is the cornerstone of the internal market. Community control of national subsidies is fundamental to that system. Indeed, aid can have the same effect as tariffs and replace the non-tariff barriers currently being dismantled. Accordingly the Commission has been reviewing its state-aid policy. In 1989 it published a First Survey of aid in the European Community, followed in July 1990 by a Second Survey. On the basis of these surveys, the Commission identified a number of areas in need of closer attention. One was the question of financial relationships between public authorities and publicly-owned companies.

The regulatory framework
In 1980 the Commission had adopted a Directive on the transparency of financial relations between the Member States and their public companies.[1] This Directive required Member States to make financial information available to the Commission for five years and to supply such information on request, to enable the latter to ascertain that no hidden aid was provided to or by Member States' public companies.

Some Member States immediately accused the Commission of discrimination against public companies, and sought a ruling from the Court of Justice on the matter. However, the Court rejected this claim, observing that

> decisions of public companies may be affected by factors of a
> different kind (than profitability) within the framework of the
> pursuit of objectives of public interest by public authorities
> which may exercise an influence over these decisions. The
> economic and financial consequences of the impact of such
> factors lead to the establishment between those companies and
> public authorities of financial relations of a special kind which
> differ from those existing between public authorities and
> private companies.

The Court thus confirmed the Commission's duty to ensure that the right of Member States to own companies and provide capital or other forms of finance was not used to circumvent state-aid rules or as a means of gaining unfair advantage. In general, private companies can only secure aid from the state through schemes which must be notified to the Commission and are subject to Community scrutiny. The situation with respect to publicly-owned companies, however, is not always clear-cut. Here the state may be acting as a shareholder, or as the provider of a subsidy - and the subsidy can be difficult to identify. In addition to benefiting from notified aid schemes in the same way as private companies, public companies can derive other advantages from their relationship with the State. They may, for example, receive a capital injection

---

1. Commission Directive 80/723/EEC, *OJ L* 195, 29 July 1980.

which would not have seemed reasonable to an investor in a private company in similar circumstances. They may be granted special tax treatment. They may receive subsidised inputs, such as cheap energy. They may have their debts written off. They may be permitted to offer a rate of return which is lower than would be accepted in the private sector. Or they may have access to cheap capital because banks take account of the fact that the state stands behind them as a lender of last resort. For all these reasons, and many more, the Commission needs access to the fullest possible information on the financial relationship between public authorities and the companies they control.

On 18 October 1991 the Commission therefore issued a communication to the Member States on the application of Articles 92 and 93 and the Commission Directive of 1980 to public companies in the manufacturing sector. This communication aims to bring more clarity and openness into the present system. It does not constitute a new policy or introduce new principles to be applied in deciding what is aid or whether it is permissible. Rather, it provides for better and more timely information so that the principles currently in force can be applied correctly.

I am convinced that by applying full transparency to the public sector and by stating in which circumstances state intervention will be taken to constitute aid, the Commission can help to ensure equality of treatment between the public and the private sectors. The Communication therefore gives a detailed explanation of the interpretation of the market-economy investor principle. This principle has been upheld by the Court of Justice and has been applied by the Commission for many years to determine whether any aid is involved in public authorities' holdings in company capital.

I must emphasise that the communication stops here. Once aid has been identified, the usual analysis and derogations continue to apply in full respect of the principle of neutrality between public and private companies. If the aid is fully compatible with Community objectives it will be approved. If not, it may still be approved, but it may be subject to conditions designed to ensure that it is used to raise productivity and competitiveness, not to sustain inefficiency or to generate unfair competition.

The issue of cross-subsidisation
The 1980 Directive aims at creating transparency in the financial relations between the Member States and their public companies. But it does not in itself create transparency *within* public companies, or prevent those which have a dominant position in one market - for example due to special or exclusive rights - from competing in other markets at unfairly low prices. This threat to fair competition became clear when the Commission partly opened up the telecommunications sector to competition. Telecommunications organisations which are sheltered from competition as regards voice telephony might use equipment and manpower dedicated to that service to provide value-added services without having to charge their clients for the cost, since this cost is borne by the telephone subscribers. The same issue exists in the postal area, where national postal and telecommunications administrations often use the

same offices, postmen and vehicles to provide both the universal letter service and courier services. To ensure a level playing-field, it is indispensable to fix clear rules which should apply to such situations and allow the Commission to act, whenever necessary, to restore fair competition conditions. I have therefore asked the Directorate-General for Competition to carry out a thorough examination of this issue and to consider possible measures which could be taken to deal with it.

"Unbundling" of tariffs
There is a further issue that arises where third-party access to public companies' grids or networks is granted. It is of the utmost importance that the tariffs set for this access be based on true costs. Where they are not, the owner of the grid or network is able to significantly reduce the access of other parties by setting excessive tariffs. The Commission has therefore made proposals to the Council to impose the principle of separate ("unbundled") accounts and of cost-based tariffs. For example, in the energy sector, these proposals would require vertically-integrated electricity and gas companies to "unbundle" their accounts and to reveal their true costs by "unbundling" their tariffs.

As regards rail transport, a separation of accounts is provided for between the provision of the network and the exploitation of services.

Conclusion

Over the last few years the Commission has made great progress in opening up and levelling out the market in areas reserved for national monopolies. The confirmation by the Court of the Commission's power to proceed by Directive rather than individual decision in this respect was of crucial importance and has now become an accepted legal instrument. Because of their horizontal nature, Directives achieve the basic aim of levelling playing- fields in a way that individual decisions could never do. The process of liberalisation and levelling is of great importance to the Community, because a true common market cannot exist if large areas of its service industries, which are of crucial importance to Europe's overall competitiveness, are reserved for twelve non-competing national monopolies. The continued scrutiny of exclusive rights with a critical eye must remain one of the Community's most important policies.

11. State-aid policy: adapting to change

In a fast-changing world, governments must constantly review and adapt their policies. The difficult part is to "sell" the resulting adjustments. Vested interests must be persuaded that the changes are desirable or inevitable and that to delay them will only make matters worse. The long debate about reform of the CAP proves the point: reasoned argument can, in time, overcome the most intractable obstacles to reform. Outside pressure clearly also helps.

The same factors require and condition change in competition policy, and in particular in the giving of state aid. The need for change is there. More integrated markets within the Community call for the control of state aid to be tightened up and extended into new areas for competition reasons. The prospect of Economic and Monetary Union - assuming the track ahead of the Maastricht train can be cleared, as I am confident it can - increases the need for tighter control to help countries meet the fiscal conditions for admission to the Union. A third factor demanding change is the increasingly international dimension of the control of subsidies, as seen in the European Economic Area agreement, the European Energy Charter, GATT and the OECD. The ingredient of outside pressure for change is thus present here too.

The Commission, of course, has considerable powers, conferred by the Treaty itself in this area, but must also seek acceptance for changes in state-aid policy. How? Only, it seems to me, by force of argument. It needs to convince the doubters by making its policies transparent and accepting greater accountability for its decisions.

I will focus here on changes: the move towards stricter and wider enforcement of the Community state-aid rules and the accompanying steps towards increased transparency, both to win over the opponents of change and to satisfy them and others that the new policies are being applied, and applied fairly.

Stricter enforcement

The more closely integrated markets become, the greater the trade-distorting effect of state aid and the more tightly aid needs to be controlled. This consequence of the Single European Market programme was referred to in the 1985 White Paper.[1] It is borne out by the increasingly frequent and voluble calls for strict aid control from industrial leaders and even some governments. The most fervent supporters of this tougher stance are found - not surprisingly - in

---

1. *Completing the Internal Market*, White Paper from the Commission to the European Council, June 1985, paras. 157-59.

industries, such as the steel industry, with a painful history of beggar-my-neighbour subsidisation in an integrated market. One need only go to meetings of the ECSC Consultative Committee nowadays to realise how strong this aversion to uncontrolled subsidies has become. But the expectation that the Commission will prevent unjustified aid is spreading. It can be seen from the number of complaints the competition directorate receives urging action against alleged aid, and the frequency with which decisions to authorise aid are appealed against before the Court of Justice by the competitors of the aid-recipients.

What is the Commission doing to fulfil these expectations? Action is being taken on four fronts: definitions, limitation of aid intensity, notification and reporting discipline, and reviews.

Definitions

Under this heading I include the periodic rethinking of policy on particular types of aid as well as the redefinition of the area coverage, scope, beneficiaries and the conditions of schemes.

Broadly speaking, the more likely aid is to distort competition the harder it is justify. Aid that directly contributes to a firm's production or distribution costs and is reflected in lower selling prices is the least likely to gain exemption. Over the years, the Commission has eliminated such "operating" aid in all but a few industries and limited circumstances. The industries remaining include coal and shipbuilding. Operating aid can also still be allowed in the poorest assisted areas of the Community - those qualifying for regional aid under subparagraph (a) of Article 92(3) of the EEC Treaty. A remaining field is in connection with rescues of ailing firms. I am seeking to clarify the circumstances under which operating subsidies can be provided while ailing companies are being "turned round". My policy is to strictly limit the period over which the aid can be given and to allow it only on condition that production capacity is reduced. Capacity reduction is a necessary quid pro quo for the aid: it gives something back to the competitors of the rescued firm, namely scope to expand their own market share or a reduction of pressure on their margins. Assisted areas are of course treated preferentially under my rescue-aid policy.

After operating aid, the next most near-market and hence trade-distorting type of aid is assistance for investment. Historically, investment aid has been the main incentive offered to attract investment to assisted areas. It has been a key instrument of the policy aimed at developing a thriving small and medium-sized enterprise sector, and it has been offered on an ad hoc basis to companies which have often been large, even outside assisted areas. The latter category of investment-aid scheme - called "general investment aid" because of its general, ad hoc availability, for large firms as well as small, in assisted and non-assisted areas alike - has now virtually disappeared. Where such schemes existed the Member States have been persuaded to abolish them or to limit them to assisted areas or SMEs. Governments are still free to ask the Commission to authorise ad hoc grants of investment aid - and there might conceivably be extenuating circumstances that could induce it to permit them - but general investment schemes are no longer permissible. Here I am not referring to automatic tax allowances for investment, available across the board to any firm undertaking investment. These are part of a country's general tax system and lack the specificity of state aid in the strict sense.

Returning to regional investment aid and investment aid for SMEs, I think it is reasonable to assume that their objectives can conflict. If similar incentives for investment are offered to all but the largest companies in and outside assisted areas, what is there to attract mobile investment to assisted areas? The latter are often handicapped by poor infrastructure and inadequate communication links. Given the clear need for a trade-off between regional policy and SME policy to moderate the centripetal attraction exerted by the more prosperous Member States, the Commission has recently agreed to my proposal for guidelines on SME aid. In future, investment aid for small and medium-sized enterprises in non-assisted areas will be more tightly controlled. First of all, the Commission has now defined what is a small or medium-sized firm for state-aid control purposes: an independent enterprise with not more than 250 employees and annual sales not exceeding ECU 20m (or half that figure in total assets, or "balance-sheet total"). Only firms no bigger than this will qualify for investment aid outside assisted areas. The level of aid will be limited to 7.5% of the investment cost for medium-sized companies and 15% for small companies, defined as those with up to 50 employees and up to ECU 5m turnover. The "pro-cohesion" effect of the guidelines is enhanced by the clarification that in assisted areas SMEs can be granted investment aid of a certain number of percentage points above the authorised maximum rate of regional aid.

But the effect of concentrating investment incentives on assisted areas would be nullified if the justification for areas' assisted status were not regularly reviewed. This is the Commission's practice and the result has been a reduction in the total assisted area of West Germany, for example, to 27% from 39%. Without regular attempts to reduce the area or population coverage of regional aid schemes, especially in the centrally-located countries, the constant pressure to increase them would be difficult to resist and cohesion would suffer.

Two final areas in which aid policies are being redefined in this way are research and development and environmental protection. National aid for R & D - not, of course, Community aid - is regulated by a Community Framework which dates from 1986. This lays down maximum permissible intensities for aid for basic research and for applied research and development, and defines eligible costs. The Framework has proved useful in controlling aid to such activities and no change was found necessary when it came up for review last year. However, there has been pressure to stretch the scope of the Framework downwards from development - extending to the building of pilot or demonstration plants - into activities that may go under the name of innovation but really involve normal investment. I have resisted this tendency by seeking a much clearer definition of the concepts involved in order to reduce the grey area and thus the scope for abuse.

A similar examination is now in progress with the aim of revising the Community Framework for environmental aid. This covers an increasingly important area of the Commission's state-aid work and a revision and tightening of the current rather loose guidelines has become urgent.

Intensities

As a rule, the trade-distorting effect of aid is proportionate to its level or intensity, as a percentage of the costs it helps to cover, or to its amount. State-aid control has traditionally focused more on intensity than on volume of expenditure. This is still the case today, though later I will touch on three areas where the approach is to tackle volume.

I have mentioned the maximum intensities the Commission has now laid down for aid to SMEs for investment in non-assisted areas. Regional aid has also long been subject to intensity ceilings tailored to the development needs of the individual region. As and when regional aid schemes in the more prosperous Member States have come up for review, I have sought to reduce the percentage ceilings. This is not discrimination. The fact is that unless regional aid levels at the centre of the Community are cut, the differential in investment incentives in favour of the more peripheral areas will be insignificant, for the poorer countries often cannot afford to give the levels of aid the Commission has authorised.

For example, although the Commission has proposed to authorise up to 75% investment aid for the poorest peripheral areas of Portugal, Spain and Greece, we find that, on average, their governments can afford to pay only 25-30%. This contrasts with maximum rates of 18% in West Germany, 25% in France and up to 30% in parts of the UK. Thus the real power of aid to attract inward investment relies on a very small gap between what the richest and poorest regions of the Community can afford to pay.

Maximum aid intensities are therefore an essential instrument of subsidy control. Without them, subsidy levels are gradually bid up. There is a "ratchet" effect, which is as inevitable as the blurring of definitions and dividing lines which takes place if these are not regularly revised and refined.

Although control has focused on intensities, cash limits on individual grants and total expenditure on schemes have always been taken into consideration. In future, volume control may assume increased importance. In coal aid this is already the case. Commissioner Cardoso e Cunha and I are tackling the problem by obtaining cuts in the tonnage of subsidised coal that is guaranteed a market through long-term contracts. We are working on two fronts. By cutting the amount of output which is guaranteed support, we reduce aid levels, since the most inefficient mines should be the first to close. Secondly, we also, in appropriate cases, cap the amount of aid which can be granted. This forces the mines to contribute to greater efficiency by rationalising so as to ensure that the maximum volume can be covered by the aid level set.

Two other proposals to control aid levels are under discussion. One is my own suggestion to set limits on the amount of investment expenditure that may be subsidised per new job created in capital-intensive investment projects. The other has been advanced by the Council's Economic Policy Committee. Its idea is that the Ecofin Council should monitor overall aid expenditure as part of the future multilateral supervision of Member States' budgets.

Notification and reporting discipline
Member States have become more punctilious in notifying aid to the Commission for approval. The penalties for failing to notify were sharply increased by the 1990 Boussac judgment of the Court of Justice. In this judgment the Court indicated that the Commission had the power to issue injunctions to order a Member State to cease paying aid that the Commission had not authorised. Last year the Commission used this power over the French racecourse-betting monopoly, the PMU. The power of injunctive relief is a significant addition to the arsenal of the Commission in combatting unnotified aid, reinforcing as it does that of the retrospective recovery of illegal aid.

Notification discipline ensures that the Commission sees and evaluates aid. But once authorised the operation of aid schemes should be monitored. That is why I regard regular reporting as essential, and am proposing to the Commission to standardise such reports and to require them systematically.

Review
Finally, it has been one of my priorities to take a fresh look at authorised schemes after a certain time. This power of review is provided for in the Treaty - indeed it is a duty, for the Treaty states that "the Commission shall keep under constant review all systems of aid existing" in the Member States. The purpose of this provision is to ensure that aid systems are adapted to the changing situation of the internal market. For example, since 1989 we have been reviewing and abolishing general investment-aid schemes in various Member States. Such schemes can no longer be justified in an integrated market, and they also run counter to another Community priority, that of cohesion.

Wider enforcement - new fields of state-aid control

While the depth and precision of the Commission's aid control has increased, so too has its scope. Much of this extension is demand-driven. More and more complaints are being made to the competition directorate and myself about aid in sectors never before investigated, ranging from weather forecasting to football. Broadcasting, banking and insurance have become regular areas of our work. Typically, such cases involve competition between public-sector organisations and private firms, which claim that the public enterprise is cross-subsidising commercial activities. For example, private export-credit insurers complain that the official export-credit agencies compete unfairly for insurance of marketable risks. For export-credit insurance within the Community I have proposed a mechanism designed to ensure that the official agencies do not receive unfair subsidies.

Earlier this year the Commission proposed to the Council directives to begin the process of opening up national electricity and gas markets to competition. As integration progresses, aid - and I am thinking here of the electricity industry only - will need to be brought under stricter control. Security of supply is no longer any excuse for protecting indigenous energy resources, through aid or otherwise, on the scale that has been customary hitherto. I have agreed with the Energy Commissioner that there should be a limit of the equivalent of 20% of electricity consumption. The rest of a country's energy requirements should be drawn from the open market without subsidies or other protection. By the end of the century the protected sector should be down to 15%. This means that Member States which have domestic energy sources can choose to protect one of them (or more if they are lucky enough to have several), by a variety of means such as aid, exclusive supply contracts, and levies on consumers, within the limits set by the Commission. For example, the UK has chosen to use its 20% to protect its nuclear sector and Germany and Spain their coal sectors. Limited protection of national energy sources contributes to Community security of supply, but the counterbalance is provided by the fact that 80-85% of the market must be opened up to intra-EC competition.

Two other expanding areas of state-aid work are privatisation and the monitoring of financial transfers to nationalised firms. I have discussed the latter at length in an earlier chapter. Privatisation can involve aid in many forms or be entirely free of aid. It needs to be closely vetted, especially when firms are being relieved of debt. The Treuhand privatisations in East Germany are the largest such exercise the Commission has yet had to deal with. Here the Commission has sought to ensure that the process of conversion from a command to a market economy proceeds without discrimination (so we insist on sales by open bids) or undue aid. Massive aid is certainly needed in the new Länder, but we must ensure that it does not unduly disadvantage competitors in other parts of the Community. We have taken particular care in sensitive sectors such as steel, shipbuilding and cars.

Freedom of information, the basis of consensus

Acceptance of a policy is founded on information. Public support for strict state-aid control has grown in recent years. Some countries can be relied upon to side with the Commission on most state-aid issues. Nevertheless, doubters remain and all countries need to be shown that the Commission is dealing fairly with them. Feelings of being the object of discrimination are aroused easily and dispelled with difficulty. That is why I attach the utmost importance to transparency of policy and decision-making. Information builds consensus.

Since becoming Commissioner I have held regular multilateral meetings with Member States to discuss state-aid matters. A discussion document reformulating policy in a given area is on the agenda of each such meeting. For example, draft policy guidelines or frameworks are regularly discussed with the Member States - often several times - at such gatherings before the Commission issues them.

Statements of policy of this nature are a key element of transparency. But they are much more - they are a vital ingredient of policy-making itself. And afterwards they help the Commission to hold a consistent line.

The guidelines on state aid for small and medium-sized enterprises are the latest addition to these frames of reference. Frameworks on restructuring and rescue aid, on export-credit insurance and capital-intensive investment are in the pipeline, joining the existing codes on R & D, environmental aid and aid to the car, steel, shipbuilding, synthetic fibre and coal industries.

The Commission takes too many decisions on state-aid matters each year for all to be reported in full. But even the smallest cases that are decided summarily by the Commission are reported briefly in the EC's Official Journal and decisions on cases that "go to trial" are published in full. A large section of the Commission's annual report on competition policy is devoted to state aid, too. So information is available and I have the impression that our policies are becoming more widely understood as a result.

The Commission is sometimes portrayed as lacking accountability for its decisions. This assumption is misleading. There is a difference between being subordinate to another body in decision-making and being accountable. The former is not what the Treaty provides for, subject of course to judicial review by the European Court of Justice, which means that the Commission must always explain the reasoning behind its decisions so that it can be challenged if interested parties do not share it.

I have to defend my proposals - and later the Commission's decisions - to my fellow Commissioners, to the European Parliament, to the Council and individual national ministers, to the press and on television. And we are increasingly taken to Court. The judicial review of the Commission decisions in state-aid matters is soon to be strengthened. The Court of First Instance is to be given jurisdiction to hear appeals by private parties against state-aid decisions. Both decisions to ban and to authorise aid are open to attack. I welcome this extra tier of judicial control and am confident the Court of First Instance will accomplish its new task in as admirable a way as the Court of Justice has done.

I do not fear comment, or criticism, or judicial review because I think we are winning the argument that a reinforced state-aid policy is necessary for the Single Market and actually in the interest of European industry. A properly-enforced competition and subsidy policy, showing flexibility where warranted and necessary, is the best guarantee of future competitiveness and prosperity.

12. Subsidiarity in competition law and the Notice on National Courts

The principle of subsidiarity is neither new to Community law nor an invention of the Commission and the Council as a response to the Danish referendum rejecting the Maastricht Treaty. Indeed, the draft notice on the application of Articles 85 and 86 by national courts was published long before "subsidiarity" had become a household word.

In reality subsidiarity is at the heart of Community competition law. Given the present interest in this legal and political principle, I propose to consider not only the national courts notice, but also the wider issues of subsidiarity and competition law.

The concept of subsidiarity is the base upon which the jurisdictional divide between the Community and the Member States is constructed in competition law. In analysing its practical impact two separate issues must be considered: firstly, what should be the proper legal limits of the Commission's jurisdiction? and secondly, how can those limits, once set, themselves be implemented in a manner consistent with the principle of subsidiarity?

The first of these questions can be answered rather easily. Action at the Community level is required where national measures would not adequately address one of the Community's fundamental aims, set out in Article 3(f) of the Rome Treaty, namely the creation and maintenance of a system that ensures that "competition in the internal market is not distorted".

To achieve this aim, action by the Commission is vital. Agreements, practices and mergers that have Community-wide effects require a Community-wide analysis. The focus of this analysis at national level would inevitably be limited to the territory of the country concerned. A merger, for example, should be prohibited only if it results in an unacceptable degree of market power on the relevant geographical and product markets, which must be defined according to economic criteria. To look at a merger's effects in a single Member State when its effects and true economic context are Community-wide would lead to incorrect and unreliable decisions. This is equally true of Community-wide cartels and abuses of dominant position aimed at excluding competitors from other markets.

Furthermore, the importance of fact-finding at the Community level should not be underestimated. A Europe-wide cartel can only be adequately investigated by the Commission. The plastics cartel cases provide excellent examples of this. Equally, the basis of any analysis of the effects of a merger on competition rests on a determination of the existence of substitutes for the products or services of the merging firms. A regulatory authority must identify the actual and potential competitors of the merging firms to determine the extent of their market power. This requires analysis of a number of structural factors and detailed market research. It is of crucial importance to take into account the views of those directly affected by the merger; potential substitute suppliers for the goods of the merging firms are often situated outside a single Member State, as are potential customers. To limit research into the effects of a merger to a single Member State in such circumstances would lead to incomplete data and thus to unreliable decisions. In this respect, the need for a regulatory body with the mandate and the skills to undertake such tasks is clear. The Commission is simply the only body with the experience, the resources, the languages and the Treaty-based responsibilities to carry out these difficult cross-border analyses.

On the other hand, in cases where the effects of a merger, an agreement or an anti-competitive practice are limited entirely to a single Member State, it may be that the problem can be adequately dealt with by that country's competition authority. In such circumstances the Treaty's objective in Article 3(f) can be attained by measures taken at national level and the Community should refrain from acting. The Treaty therefore provides that Articles 85 and 86 can only be invoked where the agreement or practice in question affects trade between Member States. The Court of Justice has interpreted this to mean that an *appreciable* effect on trade must be identified, not simply a theoretical one.

This applies equally to state aid, much of which is given to protect a firm from outside competition, to promote exports to other areas or to attract mobile international investment. In an internal market with no boundaries to impede the free movement of goods and services, aid to companies in one area can have a direct and devastating effect on competitors in other parts of the market. Obviously, Member States cannot be expected to take account of the external impact of their policies and an independent referee is needed to ensure fair play. That is why the Treaty made the Commission responsible for controlling state aid. In order to prevent the richer regions outbidding their poorer neighbours, to avoid retaliatory aid and to assure Member States that they do not need border controls in order to ensure fair competition, the Commission must exercise even-handed control over all national aid policies.

However, the Commission is only responsible for state aid which affects intra-Community trade. It is not for us to say whether the local Council may give the local baker a grant to extend his premises or change his shop-front. In May 1992 the Commission adopted a proposal I had made to introduce a *de minimis* rule for state aid. It is clear that below a certain level, aid granted to companies cannot be said to affect the Community-wide market. After discussion with the Member States we have set this level at 50,000 ECU paid over any 3-year period.

The Merger Regulation is a particularly good example of how the subsidiarity principle has been used to provide an appropriate balance between action at the Community and at the national level. The Regulation's adoption, after 16 years of negotiation, was in itself a recognition by the Member States that common action was necessary to provide an efficient regulatory mechanism to vet the increasing number of mergers and acquisitions that have truly Community-wide consequences.

Concentrations between companies that meet the thresholds set out in Article 1 of the Regulation fall within the exclusive jurisdiction of the Commission, while the competition authorities of the Member States are responsible for those below the thresholds. The thresholds themselves are designed in such a way that mergers between large firms, that will usually have economic effects throughout the Community, come under the Regulation. Those between smaller firms, which have no or very limited effects in other Member States, are outside its scope. It is true that the thresholds are too high at present to include in the Community's jurisdiction all concentrations having Community-wide effects, and my department is examining carefully at what level the thresholds should be set in order best to reflect their underlying objective. This does not, however, detract from the fact that the underlying rationale of the thresholds is the subsidiarity principle itself.

Furthermore, it is notable that when the Regulation was adopted the Commission not only acquired new powers, but also explicitly and intentionally accepted that it should give up other powers it had previously held. The Continental Can judgment of 1972 confirmed the Commission's jurisdiction to prohibit concentrations that strengthened a dominant position. The only limit to this jurisdiction was that the Commission had to demonstrate the existence of an effect on trade between Member States. However, when negotiating the Regulation with the Council I recognised that it was necessary for the Commission to cede its jurisdiction for those concentrations below the thresholds. The need for the single regulatory-control principle to apply both above and below the thresholds, with the considerable benefits to industry that results from this, meant that such a readjustment of jurisdiction was necessary. I therefore proposed that the Council Regulations implementing Article 86 should not apply to concentrations. As a consequence of this, the Commission has *lost* the power to take effective measures regarding mergers and acquisitions that do not meet the thresholds of the Regulation. On the other hand, it has clearly acquired the jurisdiction and procedural means to vet those mergers with respect to which Community action is indispensable.

The second question, that of how these limits, once set, can themselves be implemented in a manner consistent with the principle of subsidiarity, is somewhat more difficult.

In relation to mergers, the Regulation admits that the use of thresholds alone will never guarantee that subsidiarity is fully respected in every single case. They are a compromise between the need to reflect their underlying objective and the requirement that they be readily understandable and easy to apply in the real world. It is inevitable, therefore, that no matter where the thresholds are set, there will be cases where mergers that have effects throughout the Community fall below them. There will also be cases where mergers that have effects limited to a single Member State nonetheless meet the thresholds.

The Regulation therefore contains two referral provisions. The first of these enables the Commission to refer to a Member State any case that is notified to it but which raises serious competition issues that are limited solely to that country's territory. The second enables a Member State to refer to the Commission those concentrations below the thresholds that nonetheless have Community-wide effects.

The provision for referral to a Member State has already been considered in individual cases a number of times. I will look at two cases, *Alcatel/AEG-Kabel* and *Tarmac/Steetley*, which provide excellent examples of subsidiarity in practice.

The first case concerned the purchase by Alcatel of AEG's cable business in Germany. The acquisition was notified to the Commission. The Federal Cartel Office in Berlin feared that the merger would create a dominant position for telecommunications cables in Germany. The Commission examined the matter carefully, but concluded that for those products the geographical market on which the impact of the merger needed to be judged was the Community as a whole. Deutsche Telekom already had a Community-wide purchasing policy, and no significant specification requirements existed which would exclude any non-German supplier. We therefore refused to refer this case to Germany, as it was a matter most appropriately dealt with at the Community level.

The Tarmac/Steetley case concerned the proposed merger of the building-materials interests of two British companies. Although the turnover of the companies in question brought the case within the Commission's jurisdiction, a close examination showed that serious competition issues existed, but were limited entirely to local or regional areas of the United Kingdom. Whilst a risk did exist that the merger would create a dominant position in these areas, for example in the market for bricks in the North-East of England, it would not have had any effect in any other country. The United Kingdom government requested that the case be referred to it for consideration under domestic competition law. It seemed to me that this was a case where the competition problem raised did not require Community action. The application of national law would guarantee the Treaty's aim of maintaining competitive markets through the Community. It was therefore one in which the proper exercise of the subsidiarity principle required that the case be referred to the United Kingdom. For the Commission to have retained the case and attempted to remedy the problems itself would have been the response of an institution intent on expanding its jurisdiction into an area which is the proper responsibility of national government. This would be wholly incompatible with the subsidiarity principle and I therefore had no difficulty in deciding to refer the case to London. I would add that this decision was taken quite a while before the Danish referendum.

Returning to Articles 85 and 86 of the EEC Treaty, it is true that during the formative years of Community competition policy there was a tendency towards centralising their application with the Commission in Brussels. Enforcement of EC competition rules was therefore regarded as primarily a matter for the Commission, even though in legal terms there was always scope for action for national courts and authorities.

This attitude is now changing. It was certainly justified in the early days when the importance of competition policy as a fundamental tool for the achievement of an open and competitive internal market was not recognised and accepted in all Member States. Therefore it had to be the Commission's task to ensure the acceptance of this principle. Equally, until recently only a few Member States had any experience in competition matters. Some did not even have any anti-trust laws. The centralisation of enforcement was also justified because adequate case-law had to develop, under the control of the Court of Justice, which could then serve as guidelines for Member-State enforcement of Community competition rules and national court action by individual companies. Any other approach would have severely endangered the aim of creating a Community competition policy that is applied in the same way whichever administration or court is examining the case.

But it would seem to me that this attitude may no longer be justified. The importance of an effective competition policy has come to be accepted throughout the Community. Recognition is therefore growing that it is preferable for cases with a largely local or national impact to be dealt with at a national level, either through the application of EC competition rules at national level or through national competition law. This may even be appropriate when the agreement in question has some influence on trade between Member States and could therefore come under Community jurisdiction. The national authorities have all the advantages of detailed knowledge of national or local markets, are closer to the facts and will frequently be able to deal more quickly with the issues raised.

I have therefore instructed my department to examine how complaints involving agreements or practices that fall under the jurisdiction of both the Commission and one or more Member-State authorities can be best pursued. The Commission may consider that national authorities are in a better position to handle complaints concerning infringements which do not have ramifications in several Member States or which lack sufficient Community interest. It could leave the handling of these cases to the national authorities. The latter have then an option to apply either Articles 85 and 86 of the EC Treaty or their own national competition law or both.

The Commission may also want to advise complainants to address themselves to national courts. The latter are indeed obliged, when called upon, to apply Articles 85 and 86 in private litigation. Besides, they can award damages, which is something the Commission cannot do. Of course, there is the problem of the costs of the proceedings. Commission proceedings are free of charge but in some Member States, like the UK, courts can award costs. I should think that at least in such a situation, court proceedings may present an attractive alternative. I await with great interest the ruling of the Court of First Instance in a case where the Commission has rejected a complaint on the ground that national courts were in a position to provide the complainant with adequate relief.

With respect to notified agreements, the increase in enforcement under national competition laws, whilst welcome, has the disadvantage of multiple form-filling requirements, and this development must not be ignored. Perhaps we should start thinking about a single type of notification form. In addition, where the notified agreements appear to be in violation of Article 85, a mechanism might be envisaged that would enable the Commission and the Member-State authorities to consult each other on cases of overlapping jurisdiction and decide which authority is more appropriate to deal with the issue in the particular case at hand. I believe that, given the excellent working relationships that we have with the various national competition authorities, such a mechanism would contribute significantly to minimising the cost of effective anti-trust enforcement in the Community.

In order to avoid any possible misunderstanding, however, I would make clear that the Commission certainly does not intend to refrain from acting in all cases, and that I recognise the need to consider and deal with the dangers which may go along with such decentralised application. It is therefore important that this concept be handled in a flexible way.

The Commission will continue to be active in many situations, for example, where large-scale cross-border activities of firms are at stake, as in cases of price and market-sharing cartels between large European producers. The Commission must certainly also live up to its task of providing guidance to companies and their lawyers by taking decisions in areas where case-law is as yet undeveloped.

Equally, it is not the Commission's intention that a situation should develop where the uniform application of the Community's competition rules would no longer be guaranteed. On the contrary, we must seek a clear-cut framework within which the scope of activity of national judges and the role they play will become enhanced. I have already mentioned one part of the framework, namely the existing rules and regulations as implemented by the case-law of the Commission and confirmed by the Court of Justice. The other part of the framework must consist of a clear understanding by the national judges of their powers, and a recognition that they can count on the co-operation of the Commission.

It is with this in mind that my department has published a draft notice on the application of Articles 85 and 86 of the EEC Treaty by national judges. This draft is meant to be a basis for discussion and has been widely circulated. We are in the process of collecting observations and hope, on their basis, to come out with a final notice by the end of 1992.

Our intention is to encourage companies to take their cases to national courts. I have already outlined the main advantages we see in this approach. Companies, in particular complainants, will often find adequate relief before national courts from the anti-competitive behaviour of their rivals. One of the main problems likely to be raised in this context is obviously the monopoly of granting individual exemptions, which rests with the Commission. This monopoly precludes a national judge from treating a restrictive agreement as valid if it has not been subject to the scrutiny of the Commission. In the notice we propose a pragmatic and co-operative solution to this problem, with the Commission being at the disposal of the national judge for any information he or she may need. And obviously we do not propose to remain passive with respect to notifications, nor shall we fail to initiate ex officio proceedings where the need arises. The need is to strike the appropriate balance and, I hope, the national courts notice will strengthen the awareness of the need for lawyers and judges throughout the Community to play their part in the Community's competition policy.

In relation to state aid, subsidiarity plays a lesser role in the enforcement of the Treaty's competition rules. This is inevitable, because an authority cannot police itself. The role of the Commission in this respect must therefore be to ensure the maximum degree of clarity and to set outer limits within which Member States are free to decide and to tailor their own priorities to their own needs. For example, in dealing with regional aid, the Commission indicates according to objective criteria which regions may benefit and the maximum level that may be paid. While regional aid can help to develop less well-off regions even in the richest Member States, the Commission must also consider the impact this aid will have on the poorest Member States. Although the Commission authorises countries like Portugal and Greece to pay up to 75% investment aid, in practice they can only afford to pay around 25-30% on average. This may be compared to maxima of 18% in West Germany and 25% in France. It is hard for these peripheral areas to attract inward investment or to develop an indigenous economic infrastructure. Therefore in assessing regional aid the Commission must strike a balance between national and Community interests and at the same time allow the process of granting regional aid to go on at the local level where it is justified.

Similar systems apply with respect to aid for research and development. The Commission, after discussing the issues with the Member States, lays down general rules which must be respected in order to ensure that the common interest of all in fair competition is assured. Then it is up to the Member States to operate their own policies within these common rules.

Conclusion

Article 3b of the Maastricht Treaty reads:

> The Community shall act within the limits of the powers conferred on it by this Treaty and of the objectives assigned to it therein. In areas which do not fall within its exclusive competence, the Community shall take action, in accordance with the principle of subsidiarity, only if and insofar as the objectives of the proposed action cannot be sufficiently achieved by Member States and can therefore, by reason of the scale or effects of the proposed action, be better achieved by the Community. Any action by the Community shall not go beyond that which is necessary to achieve the objective of this Treaty.

I have attempted to demonstrate that Community competition policy is based, both in terms of law and practice, on subsidiarity. This does not mean, however, that Article 3b is not relevant to my portfolio.

Article 3b places a legally-binding limitation on the scope of Community action. It applies without caveat, limitation or exception. Once the Treaty has come into effect, every single new legislative act of the Community can be held up and judged under this standard. Member States and Community institutions will have the right to challenge Community measures to ensure both that they are proportionate to their objective and that the objective is a legitimate one for the Community to be pursuing.

As pointed out by the European Council in Lisbon, this will require the Community to be particularly aware of the need to restrict its intervention when proposing new legislation, and to be particularly vigilant when exercising its powers in individual cases. The prospect of the entry into force of Article 3b has provided an impetus for once again examining whether the existing jurisdictional balance between the Community and the Member States remains appropriate. This is as true for competition policy as it is for any area of the Commission's business.

Edmund Burke considered that a state without the means of some change is without the means of its own conservation, and in applying the principle of subsidiarity to Community law, we must be aware of the need to be adaptable to change. The world does not stand still, and with the rapid social, economic and technical changes that characterise our society we must be willing to constantly ask the question: what must be done through common action, and what can be achieved by national, or indeed regional governments?

There has been much change in the Community since 1957, and the pace of change has increased in recent years. We have reacted, and must continue to react, to these changes in the field of competition policy. The markets of the Community have been integrating at an extraordinary pace, giving rise to an ever-increasing number of agreements and mergers that require examination at the Community level. The effective enforcement of competition policy at the national level has become the norm, not the exception. The Merger Regulation, which involved a redistribution of powers between the Community and the Member States, such that the Commission both acquired and gave up powers, is an example of this adaptation to change.

With the introduction of the principle of subsidiarity as a binding legal norm, indeed a constitutional requirement, we must continue to follow this approach. In the debate over Maastricht the Commission will without doubt be accused of talking about subsidiarity, but doing nothing more. The history of Community competition policy enforcement, which has involved the increase of the Commission's powers in some areas and their decrease in others, and the fact that this process is a continually-evolving one, gives the lie to such cynicism.

13. A look to the future

A vision of how the Community's competition policy will develop over the coming years requires the examination of two distinct sets of issues. The first falls within the category of those constants that have characterised the policy since its inception. It concerns the wholehearted pursuit of cartels, exclusive or predatory abuses, and parallel import restrictions. These anti-competitive agreements can be dealt with rather simply. The battle against them will continue to form the backbone of the Community's competition policy. There can be no higher priority for an anti-trust agency than their detection, their elimination and their deterrence.

There may, in time, be an evolution of our policy on agreements preventing parallel trade. When the common market has become integrated to such an extent that differential pricing between different areas of the Community is no longer an economically-viable proposition, the need to take a strict view of such market-distorting practices could become less, or even obsolete. I think, however, we are still a considerable number of years away from that point.

In relation to the other types of agreement or practice that I have mentioned, I can conceive of no development, be it political or economic, that could change our view that they are contrary to the fundamental aims of the Treaty. Each year, the illegality of these practices becomes better known, and the law ever more certain. Excuses or mitigating factors therefore become fewer and less credible. Over the past ten years there has been a continual increase in the level of fines imposed on cartels and abuses of dominant positions. I see no reason to expect that this trend will be reversed.

Competition policy and the evolution of the Community

The second set of issues concerns those areas of Community competition policy that are likely to evolve with the rapidly-changing nature of the Community itself. Leaving aside the short-term political difficulties of Maastricht, a number of important forces can be identified which will have a major impact on many aspects of competition policy. They are cohesion; enlargement; the globalisation of markets; economic and monetary union and economic convergence; and the continued need to respect the principle of subsidiarity.

I am not suggesting that we will see fundamental and overnight changes in either the objectives or the application of competition policy as a result of these forces. Rather, the policy must adapt to accommodate and respond to them if it is to remain the vital element of Community policy it is today.

Subsidiarity

I have not as yet explicitly discussed the role of this principle in Community competition policy. But in the light of the questions raised earlier in this book, it is evident that subsidiarity has always been the central pillar upon which the jurisdictional divide between the Community and its Member States in the field of competition policy is based.

Article 3b of the Maastricht Treaty has been quoted above on the subject of subsidiarity. As regards competition policy, the application of this general principle is relatively simple. The objective to be achieved is set out in Article 3(f) of the Treaty of Rome: the creation and maintenance of "a system ensuring that competition in the internal market is not distorted". This objective in itself has two underlying aims, the establishment of a level playing-field throughout the Community, and the creation of market conditions that will lead to growth and prosperity.

These aims can, in many cases, be achieved only by regulatory control at the Community level. Mergers, for example, that have effects in more than one Member State or with respect to which the relevant geographical market is Community-wide, can only be effectively examined by a body that has the tools, both fact-finding and linguistic, to place the operation in its correct context. This is not an issue of ideology, but one of basic economics. To correctly assess the effects of a merger or acquisition it is necessary that the relevant market be correctly defined. To do this one must not only examine a number of objective factors but also elicit the views of those affected by the operation in question. In the case of mergers with effects wider than a single Member State, those companies may be scattered throughout the Community. In many cases they will be from outside the Community. The failure adequately to take these factors into account will lead to incomplete information and unreliable decision-making. The realisation that the control of such operations at the Community level was necessary is in fact the basic reason for the adoption of the Merger Regulation by the Council in 1989.

The same reasoning applies to many other areas of competition law where, no matter how efficient, control at the national level will not achieve the objective of Article 3(f). Joint ventures between companies in different Member States, Community-wide cartels, abuses of dominant positions aimed at market separation or foreclosure, and distribution agreements that prevent parallel trade provide clear examples of operations that can only be satisfactorily examined at the Community level.

State aid deserves a special mention in this respect. Aid is often given to shelter a national industry from competition coming from other Member States. Such support represents one of the most serious restrictions of competition in the protectionist's armoury. Each time aid is granted in one Member State, industries in others - perhaps more efficient - are put at a disadvantage. The only logical response would be to raise tariff barriers or to impose countervailing duties - actions which are fundamentally incompatible with the common market - or to grant competing aid. The resultant "aid wars" would help no-one, least of all the consumer. It is clear, therefore, that Community control is necessary. It is unrealistic to expect Member States to police themselves, and in any event a Member State itself cannot prevent other countries from granting aid to the disadvantage of its industry.

All of this, however, does not mean that subsidiarity has no role to play in the Community's competition policy. In fact it has played a guiding role ever since the signing of the European Coal and Steel Treaty. The Community has jurisdiction to act when an agreement, a practice or an instance of state aid has an appreciable effect on trade between Member States. Where the economic effects of an operation are limited entirely to a single Member State, it is normally most appropriately dealt with by the national competition authority, and thus the Commission has no jurisdiction in such cases. The Merger Regulation also reflects this. The thresholds are designed to bring within the Commission's exclusive jurisdiction those operations between large firms that almost inevitably have Community-wide effects. Mergers between smaller companies, less likely to require a Community-wide analysis, fall to the exclusive jurisdiction of the Member States. The referral provisions, Article 9 and 22(3), provide a flexible method of refining this rather crude divide.

Furthermore, all of this does not mean that subsidiarity has no role to play in the future development of Community competition policy. On the contrary, with the introduction of Article 3b it becomes not just a guiding principle, but a legal norm. In future, all Community acts may be held up and compared to its standard by the Court of Justice.

The challenge facing us is to continue to find the correct balance: the Community acquiring the sole jurisdiction to vet those mergers, agreements and practices that cannot, or will not, be effectively regulated at the national level, and the national authorities acquiring the sole jurisdiction to examine those operations the effects of which are limited to their national territory. This is by no means an easy judgment, as it rests on a series of factors that are themselves constantly changing. For example, the internal market leads to companies adopting Community-wide marketing and production strategies. As a consequence, the seemingly-inexorable growth in mergers and joint ventures and Community-wide distribution agreements that *must* be dealt with by the Commission, if they are to be judged on the basis of sound economic evidence, will continue to grow.

On the other hand, because of the lack of effective regulatory control in many Member States, the Commission has in the past had to take a leading role in cases which, whilst they affected trade between Member States and thus fell within the Commission's jurisdiction, could in economic terms have been dealt with adequately by a national court or a national regulatory authority. If the Commission had refrained from acting in such cases, many anti-competitive agreements or practices would have been tolerated. The Treaty objectives would not have been achieved, customers would have been exploited and the common market would have been fragmented by privately-erected entry barriers. This, however, has now changed to a significant extent, and is continuing to do so. Effective anti-trust enforcement now exists in a significant number of Member States and we are therefore seeing the first signs of what may be a rather long-term process, the achievement of the Community's objectives through co-ordination and partnership involving regulation at the Community and national levels. I say long-term, because the degree and nature of enforcement throughout the Community still varies enormously - in the Netherlands, for example, there is no effective anti-trust policy.

Nonetheless, the Community must already react to these changes, and aside from encouraging greater application of Articles 85 and 86 in national courts, the Commission is examining how complaints involving agreements or practices that fall under the jurisdiction of both the Commission and one or more Member-State authority can best be pursued. The Commission may consider that national authorities are in a better position to handle complaints concerning infringements which do not have ramifications in several Member States or which lack sufficient Community interest. Where a Member State applies effective competition law, the Commission may therefore refrain from acting so that the case may be dealt with by the national authority applying either Articles 85 and 86 or its own national competition laws.

Thus, the implementation of Article 3(b) over the coming years will require an openness to change on the part of both the Commission and the Member States, for gradual but constant change is a direct consequence of the application of subsidiarity.

Convergence and cohesion

One important factor that will shape competition policy in the future, and in particular influence national policies on state aid and the role and size of the public sector, is the decision to move to Economic and Monetary Union and the need for the different economies of the Community to converge. In drawing up their economic and fiscal programmes to take account of the agreed convergence criteria and the need to avoid excessive budget deficits, all Member States will have to decide on the volume of resources which can be devoted to state aid and financing the public sector. Some expenditure, such as that on health, education and the unemployed, is unavoidable and socially desirable. Other expenditure is more discretionary and Member States may find that policy objectives can be met by means other than granting subsidies to industry.

Member States with large budget deficits will have to pay particular attention to the size of their aid budgets. As part of its drive to reduce state aid, which distorts competition in the internal market, the Commission will be pressing for the elimination of certain aid systems. For example, we have encouraged a number of Member States to abolish general investment aid, which is anti-competitive and anti-cohesion.

However, it will almost certainly be the case that Member States will be obliged to cut back on spending on aid systems even where the Commission, under its state-aid policy, would authorise them. For example, Member States, in choosing between competing priorities, may decide to reduce spending on direct subsidies or to reduce the budget allocated to particular schemes. To take a specific case, Italy has a large budget deficit of which 28% is accounted for by state aid. It has launched a scheme of aid for SMEs which has a budget of 1bn

ECU - a large sum by any standards and considerably more than is allocated for such purposes in Member States which do not have similar deficit problems. It is possible that in the context of the austerity programme which Italy will have to implement in order to meet the agreed EMU targets, such programmes will have to be scaled down even though the objective of promoting the development of SMEs is in itself worthy and deserving of a favourable attitude from the Commission.

In this context, the EcoFin Council will have to be demanding in terms of the targets it agrees and strict in ensuring that they are met. In future it will not just be intra-EC competition which will be adversely affected by excessive spending on state aid, but the stability of EMU itself.

Let me now turn to another area inside the Community where I see developments in competition policy - public enterprises. Member States will, over the coming years, be reviewing the size and operation of their public sectors, particularly when public companies are involved in economic activities which can also be undertaken by the private sector. I do not wish to enter a debate about the philosophy of public ownership. This is an area where debate is coloured by ideology. The balance is for the Member States to decide in the proper exercise of subsidiarity. I am just pointing out that the weight of the public sector in public finance will, at least in certain Member States, need to be considered and that the results of the review process will have repercussions for competition policy.

In our state-aid policy we have had to address the question of public companies. Public and private companies compete directly in many product and service sectors. It would be a serious distortion of competition if public companies were to receive advantages from their special relationship with the public authorities which were not available to private companies. It would be equally improper to deny to public companies the aid available to private companies. Moreover, given that the mix of public and private companies is different in each Member State, a situation which allowed for different treatment based on ownership of companies competing for the same customers would very quickly lead the Member States to call into question the basic trust which allows the internal market to function. Take the example of steel. This is a commodity, for the most part, for which the relevant market is not national but the Community as a whole. If public and private steel companies are to compete in the same market it must be on the basis of the same rules of conduct - otherwise Member States will reintroduce barriers to trade to offset the unfair advantages of grants granted to one producer and not to others.

Therefore the Commission must ensure that the financial relationship between the public authorities and public companies is transparent, and is not used to provide unfair or illegal aid. In 1991 the Commission adopted my proposal for an ex-post monitoring system for larger public companies in the manufacturing sector. The system is now starting to function and will represent an important step forward in terms of transparency and equality of treatment. Since competition between the public and the private sector is not confined to the manufacturing sector I can easily foresee the need to extend the system to other areas of economic life such as the service sector where, for example, public and private banks compete, as well as sectors such as energy, transport and telecommunications.

The second aspect I wish to discuss in relation to public enterprises concerns those enjoying special or exclusive rights - or regulated industries as they are often less accurately called. Private companies can and do have special or exclusive rights granted by governments to carry out certain functions. However, such rights are predominantly the reserve of public enterprises. Sectors such as telecommunications, post and energy are often characterised in the Community by the grant of monopoly rights.

This grant is often motivated by a belief that the industry is a natural monopoly and that competition would lead to inefficient duplication, or by the view that public enterprises are the best way to handle this monopoly, in particular where it is felt that all citizens have the right to be provided with the service in question on reasonable terms. However, these exclusive rights are at odds with nearly all the fundamental principles of the Treaty and of the Community. They preclude free competition, the freedom of establishment, and the freedom of movement of goods and services, and they deny the consumer the choice and advantages created by the internal market.

It is the Commission's responsibility in carrying out its duties under the Treaty to ensure that any such monopoly right is defined as narrowly as possible, subject to it being compatible with the provision of a service of general economic interest. This can be for example the requirement that all consumers should have access to the telephone network on reasonable terms. But such an overriding objective does not preclude other considerations. The Commission must ask itself whether the provision of certain ancillary services usually provided by the monopolist should be subject to competition. For example, can parcels or express courier services be opened up to competition whilst still preserving a universal mail service? The answer is clearly yes and competition must be permitted. This is the question that has been asked to date and applied in several cases. However, it must be increasingly supplemented by other questions, the answers to which should lead to further erosion of these monopolies.

For example, has technology evolved to such an extent that the original rationale for the monopoly is no longer valid? In the field of telecommunications, technological change means that several competing networks can easily co-exist where once it would not have been feasible. An example of this can be seen in the long-distance market in the USA, with its many competitors.

Second, one must question the assumption that a monopoly is necessary to generate sufficient revenues from certain customers to pay for connecting up poorer and disadvantaged social groups to the network, or remote regions where the costs of providing the service are greater. I would be the last person to wish to deny such groups access on equal terms to the service in question. However, the question must be asked whether there is a way of providing the service in a way less harmful to competition than through the grant of a monopoly. For example, the subsidy to connect disadvantaged groups might be made transparent. Direct subsidies may be offered on a competitive basis for firms to provide the service in question. They could bid to provide the service for the least subsidy.

The answers to such questions will form the basis of the future direction of the Community's policy on state-granted monopolies. They will have to be asked if we are not to deny the advantage of competition and the internal market to customers and businesses for several important sets of goods and services. Studies of these services in countries where competition has been introduced show that very large cost-savings can be obtained without destroying the universal service. And thus my view of the development of Community policy in this area is that liberalisation must, and will, continue apace.

Some liberalisation will result from Member States' own measures, some through Article 90, some through Article 100A. The mechanism in this respect is not as important as the result. The existence of state monopolies in sectors where competition is a realistic alternative will lead to a severe competitive handicap for those Community industries for which the monopoly services are important. Telecommunications, for example, are the life-blood of financial services and many other companies. In both Japan and the United States international telephone calls are open to competition; in the Community they are not. Unsurprisingly, of these three areas, international calls cost the most in the Community and this has given rise to the growth of traffic diversion, with EC calls being routed through the USA to make use of lower prices.

We cannot simply ignore these issues. The speed of technological change and international market-integration means that either we face them, or we accept that our inaction handicaps our own industry's competitiveness. The view that continued liberalisation must form a central part of the Community's future competition and industrial policies may not be one that is easily digestible for everybody; but it is, quite simply, inevitable.

Enlargement and the globalisation of markets
Having looked at the possible developments of competition policy inside the Community, I turn to external events and their impact. This has two aspects - enlargement of the Community and the increasing globalisation of markets. With respect to both these aspects the Community will continue to adopt an "open" attitude. Just as "open" trading was the key principle in forging the internal market that underpinned the Community's growth and prosperity, so the same "openness" will guide us in the field of international trade relations. The same economic logic of the single market applies with equal force to external trade and the globalisation of markets. The Community's political and democratic credibility and credentials oblige it to be open to other European countries. Enlargement is an immediate question as far as the EFTA countries are concerned. The question will be asked again when the East European countries become strong enough to join. I see this process of enlargement as a strengthening - not, as some have claimed, a weakening - of the Community. It is also inevitable - only the timing is in doubt. How will competition policy react?

In the first place, enlargement will make us focus even more carefully on subsidiarity. Those decisions that must be made by Brussels will be - the remainder will be for the Member States. As the number of Member States increases, the application of this principle on a practical basis will become even more crucial. However, for the many decisions that must remain with Brussels, I am convinced, not only that competition policy will be able to cope, but that its effective application is essential to successfully integrate the new Members. Competition policy has long been associated with and is indispensable for economic integration. Indeed, many Eastern European countries have adopted, and are enforcing, competition policies that many Community Member States might regard with a jealous eye. These policies will go a long way to assisting those countries to develop a vigorous market economy that should permit their entry into the Community to be seriously considered in years, not decades. Furthermore, competition policy at the Community level will remain a key policy in creating a real internal market from the separate economies of the Member States. It has coped and is coping with past enlargements, ranging from the more developed economies of Denmark and the UK to the less industrialised economies of Ireland, Greece, Spain and Portugal. It is also a key element in cohesion, which will take on increased importance whenever enlargement concerns poorer, less developed regions.

Let me now turn to the second element from outside the Community which will have an impact on competition policy - the globalisation of markets. As the world's largest trading block, Europe cannot ignore this trend, already well-advanced in certain sectors. To try to isolate ourselves would have serious implications for our growth and standard of living. The process of adjusting to internationalisation, especially in sectors undergoing rapid technological change or in traditional or declining sectors, is not always easy, but we have no choice. The alternative is no longer economically or politically feasible. Competition policy must adapt to this challenge if it is to remain as relevant as it is today.

However, whereas in the past the effects of most anti-competitive practices of companies or governments were limited to the Community, in future anti-competitive practices with an impact on our market or domestic industries, but which have their origin outside the Community, will become increasingly commonplace. The difficulty of European companies in finding adequate distribution and retailing facilities in Japan, for example, results in no small part from the very close relationships between existing Japanese distributors and manufacturers. As governmental barriers to trade come down, the relative importance of this problem will grow. Competition policy therefore becomes an instrument to establish a level playing-field at the international level. Unless companies and governments have confidence in a system of fair and undistorted competition in others' markets, pressures to re-erect trade barriers at home will strengthen.

Community competition policy has already started to react to this globalisation in several ways. First, we have considered the possibility of concluding bilateral agreements with our main trading partners. An example of this is the recent EC-US agreement. We will explore in the future whether similar bilateral agreements with other countries would be useful. Second, we have regional agreements for the application of competition rules. The most important agreements will be those with EFTA countries on the European Economic Area. In addition we have the European Agreements with Poland, Hungary and Czechoslovakia, all of which contain competition clauses. Third, we have a multilateral code of understanding in the OECD on information, consultation and co-operation between Member countries.

The use and importance of these arrangements will grow. They provide a tool that will considerably assist the move to convergence of the differing anti-trust systems worldwide. But in my view we are still lacking an essential element - a real multilateral set of competition rules. At the World Economic Forum in Davos in February 1992, I therefore suggested that the rules and procedures be strengthened in order to provide for effective enforcement under the rule of law:

> The next GATT Round should include restrictive business practices and cartels on its agenda. The aim should be to draw up common rules, lay down the principle that restrictive arrangements are not enforceable at law and that Governments are responsible internationally for the implementation of these rules and procedures. The right of recourse to GATT panels should be strengthened, as should the effectiveness of their adjudications. For mergers, common rules should also be established, as well as a common commitment to enforce them. Dispute-settlement procedures should also be strengthened.

The Community is sometimes criticised for being slow to react in trade matters. In this field we are ideally-placed to take the initiative. We have a wealth of experience in establishing and enforcing competition rules that apply to countries varying greatly both politically and economically. Our immediate task is to undertake the groundwork, by bilateral, regional and multilateral contacts or agreement, and then to table a coherent framework for bringing anti-trust activity under the GATT in the next round of negotiations. I do not pretend that it will be a simple process. But with the continual integration of markets the risk of back-door protectionism though unequal competition-policy enforcement is too great to allow ourselves to ignore this problem.

Procedures in the future
To conclude, I would like to consider perhaps the most important practical challenge that the Community faces over the coming years - that of procedure. It must be acknowledged that the Commission prohibits only a tiny proportion of those agreements that it examines. This does not reduce the need for systematic regulatory control to ensure that unacceptable agreements are prohibited and, perhaps more important, deterred from being concluded in the first place. It does mean, however, that the Commission must examine

agreements and practices within a short time and provide legal certainty in a manner placing the least possible burden on industry. This is particularly the case in relation to structural cases such as joint ventures. These operations involve substantial commitments by the companies involved, in terms of capital and of human and physical resources. It is often the case that a deal, once implemented, cannot realistically be unscrambled, and it is only reasonable for industry to expect the Commission to examine such cases within a short period of time.

The successful implementation of the Merger Regulation has demonstrated that, given the necessary resources and an appropriate legal framework, the Commission is perfectly capable of meeting this need. This can also be seen in the state-aid area, where we have succeeded in dramatically decreasing the time-scale within which decisions are adopted. However, the resources available to the Commission, and the framework established by Regulation 17, mean that our recent experience under the Merger Regulation cannot simply be transposed into Article 85 and 86 cases. This does not mean that I do not accept the need for change. I acknowledge that the Commission has failed to provide companies undertaking projects involving structural change with the quick decision-making progress and the legal certainty that they require. We are therefore examining how this objective can be achieved with the limited resources and cumbersome procedure within which we must operate.

The final details of this examination will be announced shortly. I can, however, already say that we intend to set internally-binding deadlines, which will be made public, within which the Commission will undertake to give an opinion on notifications involving structural change. Depending on the case in question, this opinion might be in the form of a "comfort" letter, a letter indicating an intention to propose the adoption of a formal exemption decision, or the announcement of an intention to send a statement of objections. This period will, of course, be short - a few months. The Directorate-General for competition will bring this new procedure into operation for all structural cases notified from 1st January 1993 onwards. I hope that it will be possible to carry out the necessary internal adjustments to bring it into effect before that date.

Moreover, this is only the beginning of a wide-ranging review of procedures. We are examining, for example, whether it is possible to develop a common notification-form for merger cases that could be filed either with the Commission or the Member-State authorities. We are also considering how procedures can be speeded up, and public deadlines introduced, for all Article 85 and 86 cases. Furthermore, Regulation 17/62, which sets out the basic rules implementing Articles 85 and 86, is now thirty years old. We are thus examining whether it needs to be modified to enable us to streamline procedures, particularly in simple cases, to give final, legally-binding and enforceable decisions within short deadlines. These are questions that I hope we can resolve in the second half of 1992, but it should not be imagined that easy solutions to these problems exist. Nonetheless, given flexibility and imagination on the part of the Commission, the Member-State authorities and the industrial sector, I have no doubt that rapid progress can be made.

Conclusion

The main lines of the future of Community competition policy have now been set, but there is scope for much further development, applying and extending the principles that we have established in a changing - indeed, a rapidly-changing - world. Competition policy in the EC will undoubtably continue to be an exciting challenge.

Index